S0-AIC-760

M
2117
.N535
v.1

NEW WINE IN OLD WINESKINS

A CONTEMPORARY CONGREGATIONAL SONG SUPPLEMENT

VOLUME 1

EDITED BY JAMES ABBINGTON

THE UNITED LIBRARY
2121 Sheridan Road
Evanston, Illinois 60201

GIA Publications, Inc.
Chicago

G-7113

Copyright © 2007 by GIA Publications, Inc.
7404 South Mason Avenue, Chicago, Illinois 60638
800-442-1358
www.giamusic.com

International copyright secured. All rights reserved.
Printed in the United States of America

Despite extensive efforts to determine the copyright ownership of the
selections included in this hymnal, at press time the source of some
material remains unknown. Believing that hymn writers ultimately
intend their creations to be sung in divine worship, we chose to include
this material with the intent that acknowledgement will be made in
future editions and appropriate royalties paid as such information
becomes available.

For information about copyright permission, go to OneLicense.net.

Cover design by Martha Chlipala

ISBN–13: 978-1-57999-685-7

2 3 4 5 6 7 8 9 10 11 12 13 14 15 16 17 18 19 20

I'm Going to Live the Life I Sing About in My Song

by
Michael Joseph Brown
Associate Professor of New Testament and Christian Origins
Emory University, Atlanta, Georgia

I. A VISION OF MINISTRY

I could rant against the perceived excesses or deficiencies of contemporary music in the African American religious community, but since others have already sought to do this, I shall largely refrain and trust that their criticisms have been well received. I am not a musicologist, nor am I attempting to "play" one in this essay. What I am attempting to provide, however, is some meager input and reflection from a participant-observer on the experience of music and worship in the contemporary Black church. I chose the title for this essay from a song made famous by Mahalia Jackson.* I did so because it struck me that what the song pointed to resonated deeply with my own experience and expectation of worship in the African American church. Music, as a cultural expression, should deepen and provide greater texture to our experience of the world. Music, as an artistic expression, should provide us with insights we might not normally come across—insights that make us more complex and, arguably, better human beings.

I am not suggesting that there is or should be some simplistic direct relationship between what we sing in church and the lives we live outside the confines of the sanctuary. Clearly, language, especially in its artistic expression, can never quite capture the totality of our yearnings as beings desiring a deeper relationship with our Creator. And yet, such poetic expressions may be better vehicles for our desires than any supposedly straightforward theological tome. In other words, through expressions like sacred music we may better express the complexity of our theological concepts than the most straightforward line in a creed or textbook. It is reported that the influential twentieth-century theologian, Karl Barth, was once asked what he considered to be the most profound theological expression ever made. He responded, "Jesus loves me! this I know, for the Bible tells me so." What sacred music does for us is cast visions and fashion metaphors whose depth can never be exhausted through analytical investigation. As Gerald Janzen ably noted, "we experience more than we know, and we know more than we can think; and we think more than we can say; and language therefore lags behind the intuitions of immediate experience."[1]

In the Sermon on the Mount, Jesus says, "Beware of practicing your piety before others in order to be seen by them; for then you have no reward from your Father in heaven" (Matt 6:1 NRSV). What Jesus says here supports what I believe to be an important standard by which a ministry of music should be judged. Jesus tells his disciples that they must "beware" of how they practice their faith. Actually, the Greek word here can also be translated as "be very careful" or "be on your guard." Thus, an alternate translation would be, "Be on guard concerning your righteousness." As the construction implies, there is a potential danger present when we do things like give money, fast, and pray (the actual practices discussed in Matthew 6). What Jesus is saying, then, is that special

* "I'm Going to Live the Life I Sing About in My Song," Words and Music by Thomas A. Dorsey, © 1941 (renewed) Warner-Tamerlane Publishing Corp. Exclusive Print Rights Administered by Alfred Publishing Co., All Rights Reserved.

attention is needed when we do these things, because if we do them without concern for their righteousness, then we do them illegitimately. When we approach the things of God, Jesus says, we must be careful that the deep spiritual dimension of the practice not be lost in the process.

Many people, even some biblical scholars, misunderstand what Jesus means here because they seem to forget that what he is expressing is a Jewish understanding of how we practice our faith. Almsgiving, fasting, and prayer are expressions of our worship of God. Unfortunately, far too many Christians see something like almsgiving as a moral issue, somewhat removed from what we consider to be worship. In truth, I think the same is true when it comes to the worship of God through song. We do not take the act to be as serious as it really is. So, what is the danger present when we consider sacred music in light of our worship of God?

The danger has to do with the fact that acts of worship, like singing, are matters of performance. They have to be done by someone. They take place before an audience. As Jesus explains it, there are two possible audiences available: (1) human beings or (2) God. What is clear from Jesus' statement is that any performance before a human audience is potentially dangerous—"before others in order to be seen by them." To avoid this danger, Jesus instructs us not to perform them before others. This is difficult, of course, when it comes to the function of sacred music. If anything, singing is a matter of "doing" or "performing," and so doing this before other human beings is almost always "for the purpose of being seen by them." The distinction Jesus wants to invoke is that between "theater" and "worship." The idea of confining the worship of God through song to God alone is impossible to do in a worship environment. The point in the Sermon on the Mount is not really whether other human beings will be present when we perform these acts, but whether the intention of the performer is to be seen by those present or by God.

If the intention of our singing is to be seen by the human audience, then the rules and expectations of the theater apply; that is, impressive scenery, individuals playing scripted parts, applause, emotional outbursts, and so on. Worship can degenerate into a mere public spectacle. By contrast, if the intended audience is God, then such considerations play only a secondary role. I have walked out of many worship services where I was uncertain about whether I had been in worship or at a Broadway show. This is precisely the point behind Jesus' statement: there is a thin line between worship and theater, and we must be careful to avoid crossing it.

When we worship, we glorify God and demonstrate our allegiance to God's vision for the world. Worship is a way of acknowledging the worthiness of God and God's vision for the world. This understanding, I think, brings us closer to what Jesus says in the Sermon and the standards by which I believe we should judge a ministry of sacred music. The significance resides in the purpose for which the task is undertaken. Singing is not just a performance. It is recognizing and endorsing God's vision for the world. Through our singing we paint a picture of what the world can be, not just a vision of what we want and do not want in our immediate circumstances. It is a world where God's will would be done. This is aptly illustrated in the hymn "How Great the Mystery of Faith," which says, "The best that we can do and say, / The utmost care of skill and art, / Are sweepers of the Spirit's way / To reach the depths of every heart." In short, through our ministry of music we worship God by recognizing and committing ourselves to God's vision of what life on earth can be.

Through our singing we also demonstrate that something is wrong with the world. God's vision for our lives and the lives of others has not been realized, and so we cast visions through song as a way of transforming the world into what God wants it to be. In short, it is fully an act of worship. Through our ministry of sacred music we participate in creating a world where God's love and will reign. We should judge our music ministry not only by what it does on Sunday mornings in service, but also in the way it commits us to the transformation of the earth into the Kingdom of God.

II. SINGING ABOUT A NEW JERUSALEM: CLAIMING THE PROPHETIC VOICE

It is difficult for a biblical scholar like myself to comment with any authority on the trends in African American sacred music. Certainly a shift of some sort has occurred. This may be coincident with a change in the social standing of many African Americans. It is probably premature to say that African Americans as a whole are wealthier, better educated, more savvy consumers, etc. However, this is certainly true for some. Could this perceptible shift in African American sacred music be the result of targeting an audience that is more affluent? Could the concerns of past generations of African American mothers and fathers no longer apply to this emerging group? Yes and no. While some concerns are not as central to the church-going African American community, others remain. To put it another way, while the spiritual which says, "I got shoes. You got shoes. All of God's children got shoes" or Shirley Caesar's assurance that "He's working it out for you" may be a less central concern for those with greater access to capital and credit, others, like the hymn which guarantees "we will understand it better by and by," still resonate in a community that struggles with ongoing issues of theodicy and ambiguity.

Many have pointed out that early African American sacred music was permeated with a prophetic consciousness. For example, Obery Hendricks underscores the central sensibilities of this music as "the prophetic functions of naming the oppressive reality and exhorting resistance to it, and the eschatological expectation of justice in this world."[2] A fundamental change in this early consciousness came at the beginning of the last century with the move from a largely agrarian African American population to a largely urban and industrial one. In many respects, this shift from Mississippi to Chicago was appropriate to Christianity, which was more of an urban movement than an agrarian one. The early church flourished not in the fields of villages like Nazareth but in the dense urban environments of Corinth, Ephesus, Alexandria, Carthage, and Rome. In fact, one of the most powerful symbols of the Christian vision of a transformed world was a city (Greek *polis*)—the new Jerusalem (Rev 21:2).

Some have argued for a distinct difference between prophetic critique and an apocalyptic worldview, but the distinction may not be as clear as we might think. The central motivating question for apocalyptic thought appears to be: is God faithful? It is an effort to make theological sense of a world that does not correspond to the promises God made to bless the faithful (e.g., Deut 28:1–4) and through them, the world (e.g., Gen 12:1–3; Isa 42:1–4). The dissonance between the vision and reality then prompts a crisis. How can the

God we worship be a God worthy of worship, when those faithful to God find themselves in such oppressive circumstances? As Eugene Boring once wrote, "It was the honor and integrity of God that was at stake, not just human selfish longing for golden streets and pearly gates" that gave rise to apocalyptic thought and literature.[3]

By contrast, the central motivating question for prophetic thought is not the faithfulness of God, but the faithfulness of human beings. Along with "thus says the Lord," the central characteristic of prophetic speech is the contingent construction of "if . . . then." Speaking on behalf of God, the prophet points to something gone wrong with the world, something that disturbs God and initiates God's response. Humans are given the option to transform their practices before final divine judgment is unleashed. Although in many respects these perspectives are intimately related, the question of God's faithfulness is not a central concern of prophetic critique.

These two perspectives—the prophetic and the apocalyptic—are merged in Revelation. The author does not call himself a prophet, but he claims this book to be a prophecy (Rev 1:3; 19:20; 22:7, 10, 18–19). The entire document is understood as the address of the risen Lord through his spokesman John. Although this work is saturated with apocalyptic images and content, it is probably safe to say that it is a fine example of early Christian prophecy. Thus, in truth, "prophetic" and "apocalyptic" are not alternatives when it comes to understanding Revelation, but a merged form of utterance that poses two questions not often put together in biblical literature.

This is where I would disagree with the analysis of the change in consciousness Hendricks advances. He says, "At its core, then, gospel music embodies the classic apocalyptic feeling of powerlessness to forestall the oppressive forces of this world which, in turn, is accompanied by a sense of resignation to ongoing social misery at the hands of oppressors until the apocalyptic 'day of the Lord.'"[4] The new Jerusalem, as envisioned in Revelation, is not something otherworldly but this-worldly. The new Jerusalem comes down from heaven, we do not ascend to it (see Rev 21:2).

The development of African American sacred music from spirituals to gospel may reflect a shift in venue from farm to factory, but the introduction of more apocalyptic elements into this musical expression did not, by necessity, mean that it had to lose its prophetic critique. Another way to frame the issue may be to say that, instead of simply naming the evil in this world for which human beings are responsible (the typical prophetic move), the development of gospel music highlights the disaffection experienced by African Americans who moved to the "promised land" and found no promise readily available. It is the introduction of the additional question "Is God faithful?" or more poignantly "Why, Lord?"

The rise of the soloist in gospel music may reflect the stark sense of individualism many felt in the teeming urban environments of Detroit, Cleveland, and Chicago. Instead of the creativity of community, the creativity of the gospel singer is found in the modernist sensibility of living a largely solitary and commodified existence even in the packed neighborhoods of the industrial North. This "solitary" turn is also reflected in the types of subjects addressed by these songs. While daily concerns were still paramount in many expressions of gospel music, their impact was clothed in a more subjective form. Personal testimony, personal crisis, and personal decision became the keystones of such artistic expression. Did this new expression of religious creativity express a profound sense of hopelessness? Maybe. Absolute resignation? No. Despite the abject conditions of an unrealized new Jerusalem, gospel music still spoke to a sense of hope in a transformed future. The central question is: what kind of transformed future does the singer or songwriter envision?

To the casual observer, like myself, it appears clear that there is little of the "prophetic" to be found in gospel music. There is a sense of something wrong in the world, but that wrong is not articulated explicitly as a critique of social systems that can and should be changed by active agents in the present. In fact, one may characterize the latest trend in gospel music to be one bordering on narcissism. Hope has been replaced by unabashed praise. Yet, is such praise really warranted given the continuing social, economic, and environmental problems that confront us? Such a question is taken up in the hymn "Woe to the Prophets." As this hymn proclaims, "Woe to the prophets, / Who God's blood-bought people deceive, / Who teach them to trust in their idols of dust, / And falsehood, not truth, to believe; / Who preach but for pay, and who lead men astray, / And daily God's Spirit do grieve." Still, hope as well as praise can be incorporated into prophetic critique, as they are in Revelation.

Brian Blount, in his book *Can I Get a Witness?* in a chapter aptly titled, "The Rap against Rome," points out that the hymnic language of Revelation is filled with critique of the Roman social order. What is more interesting for this investigation, however, is that he identifies its analogue in African American culture as rap music rather than sacred music. He says, "Rap expresses its painful view of the world through traditional and historical images that are particularly meaningful for the audience it hopes to energize and that it intends to critique."[5] If energy and critique are the hallmarks of (at least some forms of) rap music, then it is possible to fashion metaphors in music that speak to the complexity of modern life with both comfort and challenge.

The worship of God through song is never just a matter of casting a vision of plenty for all. Essential to that vision must be the recognition that there is something wrong with the present state of affairs. If "we're marching to Zion," it is only because we presently do not find ourselves living in the "beautiful city of God." African American sacred music should be an ecstatic expression of the fullness of God's vision for the world. Still, this should be a carefully nuanced articulation that recognizes this vision to be an ideal toward which we work. In this sense, language — and specifically metaphor — serves an asymptotic function by luring us closer and closer to the vision without fully exhausting it or collapsing it into a caricature of itself. To accomplish this, we need both praise and critique.

III. SINGING AS A CONVERSATION WITH GOD: ENRICHING THE TAPESTRY OF OUR RELIGIOUS EXPERIENCE

Life is not simply about problems. If we reduce life down to the challenges we face, whether internally or in the environment that surrounds us, then we overlook a large measure of what makes our lives liveable. Beauty, joy, happiness. sorrow, relatedness, solitude, love, and a host of other experiences repeatedly influence our lives from moment to moment. If we were to focus solely on those aspects of our experience that constitute specific, although repeated, instances of infelicity, then we overlook and fail to cultivate the richness of our overall journey in time. The ideal of human life, as well as that of civilization generally, is to experience as completely as possible the qualities of truth, beauty, creativity, adventure, and peace; at least according to Alfred North Whitehead.[6]

If we accept this understanding as true in the sense of our aim to conform appearance to reality, then much of our experience is lost if we focus on some experiences to the neglect (and sometimes denial) of others. Reclaiming these experiences means carrying on a larger conversation with each other and our Creator. Who cannot be affected deeply by the majesty of a hymn like "How Great Thou Art"? The "awesome wonder" expressed in this stirring musical expression inspires us to feel the grandeur of the universe we inhabit. Experiencing the tragic and the awesome wonder is what makes life a rewarding mystery; some would say that it is the very definition of beauty itself.[7] Yes, life is far too often plagued with tragedy, but it is also punctuated with experiences of joy, love, and awe.

My claim that sacred music should enrich the entire tapestry of our lives may sound to some as a contradiction of my previous assertion that African Americans should express a prophetic consciousness. I do not see them as contradictory but as complementary. In fact, such an approach would better reflect the range of material and perspectives we find in the biblical texts themselves. Joy sits alongside sorrow in our sacred text. In an interesting fashion, to say the least, they are often intertwined. Take, for example, Mary's hymnic outburst in Luke. She sings, "My soul magnifies the Lord, and my spirit rejoices in God my Savior" (Luke 1:46). This effusive expression of joy comes from a young maiden who has just found out that she is pregnant, though unmarried. This could hardly be conceived of as a moment of joy, especially in the period of the first century CE. Under normal circumstances, she could have been killed. Even in our own day, we rarely see the experience of unwed pregnancy as a reason for rejoicing, but more often as one for expressing our disappointment and pity. Of course, someone would respond that she has just found out that she is to be the mother of the Savior of the world. True. In my estimation, however, this does not cancel entirely a sense of dread that would have accompanied such a situation for a young woman living in a patriarchal society that often judged her value on the basis of her conformity to ideal virtues—one of which would be the maintenance of her sexual virtue. The rhetorical power of the Magnificat lies in the intertwining of a situation of tragedy and an expression of joy.

What gives the prophetic critique its power in many respects is that it casts a vision of a society that could be different. When the prophet articulates the "something" that is wrong with the world she does so by comparing it, even if implicitly, to an imagined world that would eradicate the "something" that is not an expression of the divine will. Again, rap music may be more helpful than contemporary gospel music in illustrating this idea. Tupac Shakur, for example, in his song "Unconditional Love," raps, "How many caskets can we witness / Before we see it's hard to live / life without God / so we must ask forgiveness?"[8] This is a biting social critique. Its implication appears to be that violence, especially in its most tragic form, is emblematic of a society operating in opposition to the divine aim. Shakur's lyrics at once reveal ugly, brutal truths, and at the same time point us to pictures of a caring God. I believe it is still possible for sacred music to do the same. Take, for example, the hymn "Help Us Accept Each Other," which says, "Teach us, O Lord, your lessons, / As in our daily life / We struggle to be human / And search for hope and faith. / Teach us to care for people, / For all, not just for some; / To love them as we find them, / Or as they may become." It at once recognizes the tragedy that pervades our world, but offers the possibility that such a situation can be redeemed.

Worship should be a far richer experience than a two-hour ego boost or a repeated recitation of a laundry list of unresolved problems. It, in fact, shapes us to be the human beings God sees in us. Along with its various components, worship is an ongoing practice of communication with God. It is sharing ourselves with our Creator and receiving into our lives what our Creator desires most for us. I say this because worship is more than simply expressing, "God, I want this," or, "Deliver me from that." When we worship, particularly in song, we are entering into a deeper relationship with the God who made us. This is what Abba Poemen, one of the desert fathers, meant when he said, "Teach your mouth to say what is in your heart."[9] As anyone who is in a long-term relationship knows, the relationship will not last long unless you find a way to explore all of those things that are in the depths of your heart. Simply telling God what we want—or praising God while neglecting concerns that are also God's concerns—is not fully participating in worship. Real worship is a dialogue, a two-way conversation, between us and God through proclamation, scripture reading, prayer, and song. As the hymn "God of Wisdom, Truth, and Beauty" proclaims, "Grant us visions ever growing, / Breath of life, eternal strength, / Mystic spirit, moving, flowing, / Filling height and depth and length."

We worship because we desire to see and participate in the vision our Creator has for us and the world. Of course, we will always have our own immediate requests and concerns. These we communicate to God in our worship as well. But this is not the end of it. Through worship we also listen attentively to God's voice as it tells us God's vision for our lives as individuals, as well as God's vision for the world we inhabit. Our experience of music in worship should assist us in seeing that vision in all of its complexity. The writer of Ephesians says, "I pray that you may have the power to comprehend, with all the saints, what is the breadth and length and height and depth, and to know the love of Christ that surpasses knowledge, so that you may be filled with all the fullness of God" (3:18–19). This, I believe, is what is meant by living the life we sing about, and what a creative and rich expression of sacred music can provide. Reflecting upon the collection of hymns in this volume, I believe deeply that it is still possible for such music to find its place among us, and to lure and challenge us to see the vision God still has for God's people.

Notes

1. Gerald Janzen, "The Old Testament in 'Process' Perspective: Proposal for a Way Forward in Biblical Theology," in *MAGNALIA DEI: The Mighty Acts of God. Essays on the Bible and Archaeology in Memory of G. Ernest Wright* (eds. Frank Moore Cross, Werner E. Lemke, and Patrick D. Miller, Jr.; Garden City: Doubleday, 1976), 492.

2. Obery M. Hendricks, Jr., "'I Am the Holy Dope Dealer': The Problem with Gospel Music Today," in *Readings in African American Church Music and Worship* (ed. James Abbington; Chicago: GIA, 2001), 564.

3. M. Eugene Boring, *Revelation*, (Louisville: Westminster John Knox, 1989) 40.

4. Hendricks, "I Am the Holy Dope Dealer," 576.

5. Brian K. Blount, *Can I Get a Witness? Reading Revelation through African American Culture* (Louisville: Westminster John Knox, 2005), 100.

6. See Alfred North Whitehead, *Adventures of Ideas* (New York: Free Press, 1933), 241–296.

7. Ibid., 252–264.

8. Quoted in Blount, *Can I Get a Witness?*, 113.

9. *The Sayings of the Desert Fathers: The Alphabetical Collection* (trans. Benedicta Ward; Kalamazoo: Cistercian, 1984), 189.

INTRODUCTION

In a lecture at the 1995 Hampton University Ministers' Conference, The Reverend Dr. J. Wendell Mapson, Jr., Pastor of the Monumental Baptist Church in Philadelphia, Pennsylvania, passionately declared that:

> The hymns . . . should be sung enthusiastically with the congregation standing. If the hymns are dead, it is because the people who sing them are dead . . . Congregational hymn singing is almost a lost art in the Black church. We allow the choir to do all the singing with their special arrangements and contemporary songs that people may enjoy, but cannot participate[.]

> This spectator worship is not the kind of worship pleasing to God. Congregational singing is in the intensive care unit breathing its last breath. Let's go back to the hymnal and resurrect those hymns of our faith, and sing them with life, and spirit, and joy . . . [1]

Of all the musical instruments that may be employed in the praise of God, the human voice has priority. Other instruments are to be used primarily in the service of the singing of God's people. Reformed theologian Karl Barth points out that singing is not an option for the people of God; it is one of the essential ministries of the church:

> The Christian church sings. It is not a choral society. Its singing is not a concert. But from inner, material necessity it sings. Singing is the highest form of human expression . . . What we can and must say quite confidently is that the church which does not sing is not the church. And where . . . it does not really sing but sighs and mumbles spasmodically, shamefacedly and with an ill grace, it can be at best only a troubled community which is not sure of its cause and of whose ministry and witness there can be no great expectation . . . The praise of God which finds its concrete culmination in the singing of the community is one of the indispensable forms of the ministry of the church.[2]

"Congregational singing is a well-known device for the temporary reduction of social alienation and for the accomplishment of an ad interim sense of community" wrote C. Eric Lincoln and Lawrence Mamiya. "In the Black church, singing together is not so much an effort to find, or to establish, a transitory community as it is the reaffirmation of a common bond that, while inviolate, has suffered the pain of separation since the last occasion of physical togetherness."[3]

Congregational singing is to be a purposeful act in worship, never merely a time-filler or a matter of routine. "By means of corporate voiced songs, a call to worship can be sounded, praise can be declared, faith can be confessed, a text from the Bible can be heralded, repentance can be invited, a prayer can be offered, and sacrifice can be encouraged," says S. Paul Schilling in his classic *The Faith We Sing*. Over an extended period of time, the church's worship is strengthened if congregational singing is utilized in service to all of these purposes.

Congregations should sing the fullness of Scripture and the times. Hymns provide the community an opportunity to express its beliefs about faith, doctrine, and the experiences of the Christian life. To be an authentic expression of faith, the beliefs embodied in the hymns must be true, based on Scripture, in keeping with the accepted doctrines of the congregation, and relevant to the people that sing them. Hymns should contribute to our spiritual formation, expressing doctrinal truths about God the Father and God's presence in the world; truths about Jesus Christ the Son and His work as Savior and Redeemer; and truths about the Holy Spirit, the Enabler and Comforter. These are the theological expressions. Theology, the study and understanding of God, is a significant part of hymnology, the study and understanding of hymns. This understanding is essential for the pastor, worship leader, and musicians who must lead the people of God in worship.

I have been extraordinarily privileged over the years to establish relationships and associations with such distinguished organizations and institutions as The Hymn Society in the United States and Canada, The Calvin Institute of Christian Worship at Calvin College in Grand Rapids, Michigan, GIA Publications in Chicago, Illinois, and others. Likewise, I have been fortunate to meet and nurture friendships with illustrious, established, renowned, and prominent hymn writers such as Carl P. Daw, Jr., Ruth Duck, Herman G. Stuempfle, Jr., Mary Louise Bringle, Brian Wren, John Bell, and others. Through these associations I have been introduced to the texts of Shirley Erena Murray, Sylvia Dunstan, Martin E. Leckebusch, Jane Parker Huber, Fred Kaan, and many others.

What I began to discover from my experiences in the African American churches I was privileged to serve was that these profound, prophetic, beautiful, and relevant texts were not being sung, and indeed were not even known. This situation is not unique to African American churches, but is symptomatic of all worshipping communities who are either addicted to the same hymns and unwilling to learn anything new, or simply unaware of texts written since the publication of their denominational hymnal. The majority of these texts have been written in the last twenty or twenty-five years and are not known in many mainline churches. Surveys of hymnody in congregations repeatedly indicate that, while new hymnals and supplements are continually being published, for the most part we sing the same old and familiar hymns. This is problematic in that it causes us to limit our ability to grow biblically, theologically, and liturgically.

When I presented my proposal for this compilation to GIA Publications, they were enthusiastic and very supportive of my vision and desire to expand, enhance, and enrich the hymnody in our churches. I did not want this to be an exclusively African American resource, but, rather, a collection of the very best of congregational song for all of the people of God.

The title *New Wine in Old Wineskins* is a twist on the original passages from the Synoptic Gospels (Matt 9:17, Mark 2:22, Luke 5:37–38). I immediately anticipated the criticism of biblical scholars and New Testament devotees when I selected the title. While in the Gospels Jesus clearly says that no one puts new wine into old wineskins, I chose to borrow that concept as a metaphor for this collection in which the "new wine" represents contemporary hymn texts written by some of today's finest hymn writers, and the "old wineskins" represent tried and true hymn tunes to which these texts have been set for immediate accessibility.

When considering the relationship between a particular text and tune, we can ask if it fits any of the following categories listed by Brain Wren in his unparalleled book *Praying Twice: The Music and Words of Congregational Song*. Some of Wren's categories can be investigated by singing different common meter, long meter, or short meter tunes to the same texts, using the metrical index of a hymnal.

> • *Disconnection*: Text and tune are strangers or nodding acquaintances. Neither has much impact on the other.

> • *Opposition*: Text and tune are at odds with each other. The most frequent North American choice for Edmund Sears's hymn "It Came upon the Midnight Clear" is CAROL, a lullaby waltz that contradicts the lyric's original (and often eviscerated) protest against war and poverty.

> • *Compatibility*: Text and tune are hospitable to each other. Some tunes are "open" to a variety of lyrics. When searching for a public-domain tune to pair with a new lyric, I often find sixteenth-, seventeenth-, and eighteenth-century tunes more accommodating than their nineteenth-century successors . . .

> • *Lift off*: A pleasing tune "carries" an undistinguished, undesirable, or archaic lyric . . .

> • *Unity*: When music is well matched to its text, "the music dramatizes, explains, underlines, 'breathes life' into the words, resulting in more meaning than the words themselves could express" and a more powerful effect than text or music alone[4] . . . Pairings like "Our God, Our Help in Ages Past" / ST. ANNE; "Amazing Grace" / AMAZING GRACE (NEW BRITAIN); and "Hark! the Herald Angels Sing" / MENDELSSOHN are nowadays widely experienced as "natural" or "inevitable."[5]

These were guiding principles throughout the selection and editing process for *New Wine in Old Wineskins*.

Unique to this collection are hymns, gospel songs, and contemporary music for congregational singing by such pioneering African American composers as Harry T. Burleigh, Charles A. Tindley, Charles P. Jones, Gladstone T. Haywood, Dr. Margaret Pleasant Douroux (the reigning queen of African American gospel hymnody), Charles Watkins, C. Eric Lincoln, J. Jefferson Cleveland, Laymon T. Hunter, Eli Wilson, Jr., Jimmy Dowell, and Eddie Robinson. One of these contemporary compositions, by Mr. Robinson, is an example of a community working together to enliven its faith through congregational singing. "We Study, We Shout, We Serve" serves as the mission statement of the New Mt. Olive Baptist Church in Ft. Lauderdale, Florida.

Brian Wren asserts "Congregational song is by nature corporate, corporeal, and inclusive; at its best, it is creedal, ecclesial, inspirational, and evangelical. Each characteristic is theologically important."[6] He continues,

Whether classical or popular, congregational song . . . should aim to be one or more of the following:

• *Formative*, shaping and modeling our faith as it tells a story within the whole story of God in Christ and draws us into the drama of God's saving love;

• *Transformative*, moving us from isolation to belonging, indifference to interest, interest to conviction, and conviction to commitment;

• *Cognitive*, giving us something to ponder and think about;

• *Educational*, teaching us something we didn't know about the Bible, the church, and Christian faith;

• *Inspirational*, lifting us out of ourselves into hope, joy, and peace.[7]

Special attention was given to including hymns which will help to fill voids in the current repertoire of hymns for the Christian year: there are hymns that address topics such as Advent, Transfiguration, Resurrection Sunday (Easter), and Pentecost. Neglected themes such as forgiveness, healing, reconciliation, unity, justice, and service were addressed, along with the more familiar topics of praise and adoration, worship, thanksgiving, assurance, and comfort. Also included in this collection are two extraordinary hymns by Mary Louise Bringle: "As the Waters Rise around Us," written as a response to the devastation caused by Hurricane Katrina, and "When Terror Streaks through Morning Skies," a succinct appeal for divine help in coping with the events of September 11, 2001.

Wren concludes his herculean work by asserting that "besides giving memorable, liturgical expression to theological themes elaborated more systematically elsewhere, the best hymns act as worthy partners to other theological work by expressing Christian faith in metaphor, epigram, and descriptive images which combine impact with economy, and whose metaphors may sometimes be cognitive, expanding our knowledge in a way inaccessible to reasoned exposition."[8]

Those whose ministry in the church involves music are fond of quoting Ephesians 5:19, "Speak to yourselves in psalms and hymns and spiritual songs . . ." Dietrich Bonhoeffer, one of the most widely read religious writers and theologians of the twentieth century, further expounded, "Our song on earth is speech. It is the sung Word. Why do Christians sing when they are together? The reason is, quite simply, because in singing together it is possible for them to speak and pray the same Word at the same time; in other words, because here they can unite in the Word."[9]

It is my sincere hope that the words and familiar music in this compilation will bless, edify, comfort, challenge, enlighten, illumine, teach, and admonish the people of God. If we are to sing and pray with spirit and understanding, we must mean what we say and sing, and know what we mean. As a seasoned citizen of the church once said, "It ain't no use singing about it if you don't do it." Perhaps more sublimely, S. Paul Schilling said, "Unless the hymns, or congregational songs used in corporate worship, express our real convictions, we might as well sing the stock market reports, the real estate ads from the daily newspaper, or a list of names from the telephone directory."[10]

May this first volume of *New Wine in Old Wineskins* serve the church by providing congregational song that is formative, transformative, cognitive, educational, and inspirational. May all who serve God's people as writers, composers, or leaders of worship and music be stirred by the intoxication of the Spirit to continue creating new hymns and to lead the people of God in new ways of expressing and living their faith.

My eternal gratitude is extended to:

- The staff of GIA Publications for their support of and work on this volume, especially Alec Harris, President; Robert Batastini, Senior Editor, ret.; Kelly Dobbs Mickus, Senior Editor; Jeff Mickus, Hymnal Coordinator; and Michael Boschert, Editorial Production Assistant; and to Martha Chlipala for the cover art.

- My brilliant colleague, Michael J. Brown, for the contribution of his introductory essay to this collection.

- My models of academic excellence for their friendship and encouragement: Don E. Saliers, C. Michael Hawn, Paul Westermeyer, Paul Richardson, John Witvliet, James H. Cone, Joyce Ann Zimmerman, Emily Brink, Barbara Day Miller, Horace C. Boyer, Carlton R. Young, Harry Eskew, and S. T. Kimbrough, Jr.

- Colleagues, administrators, and students of the Candler School of Theology for their kind support.

- Marie-Elena Grosett, whose father was Harry T. Burleigh's godson, for the original manuscripts of Mr. Burleigh.

- Daisy Ann Barlow, my mother, for her unfailing love and prayers.

—James Abbington, Editor
Atlanta, 2007

Notes

1. J. Wendell Mapson, Jr., *Strange Fire: A Study of Worship and Liturgy in the African American Church* (St. Louis, MO: Hodale Press, 1996), 85.

2. Karl Barth, *Church Dogmatics*, Vol. IV (London: Continuum Intl. Pub. Group, 2004) part 3, chapter 16, par. 72, #4.

3. C. Eric Lincoln and Lawrence H. Mamiya, *The Black Church in the African American Experience* (Durham, NC: Duke University Press, 1990), 347.

4. Hustad, Donald P. *Jubilate II: Church Music in Worship and Renewal* (Carol Stream, IL: Hope Publishing Company, 1993), 31 and 25–26.

5. Brian Wren, *Praying Twice: The Music and Words of Congregational Song* (Louisville, KY: Westminster John Knox Press, 2000), 77–78.

6. Ibid., 84.

7. Ibid., 71.

8. Ibid., 377.

9. Dietrich Bonhoeffer, *Life Together: The Classic Exploration of Faith Community* (San Francisco: HarperCollins Publishers, 1954), 59.

10. S. Paul Schilling, *The Faith We Sing* (Philadelphia: Westminster Press, 1983), 23.

1. A bet - ter day is com - ing, The
2. The boast of haugh - ty er - ror No
3. No more will an - gry na - tions In
4. No more shall lords and rul - ers Their

morn - ing draw - eth nigh, When gird - ed right with
more shall fill the land, While men en - raged, their
dead - ly con - flict meet, While chil - dren cry and
help - less vic - tims press, And bar the door a -

ho - ly might Shall o - ver - throw the wrong. When
pow'rs en - gaged, To kill their fel - low man, But
par - ents die In con - quest or de - feat, For
gainst the poor And leave them in dis - tress, But

A bet-ter day is com-ing, the morn-ing draw-eth nigh, 'Tis com-ing by and by, 'Tis com-ing by and by, and by, The wel-come dawn is has-t'ning on, 'Tis com-ing by and by, and by. by. by.

Text: Charles A. Tindley, 1851–1933
Tune: A BETTER DAY, 7 6 8 6 D with refrain; Charles A. Tindley, 1851–1933; arr. Charles A. Tindley, Jr.

2 A Prayer for Love

slow

1. Lord, let me love; let lov - ing be the sym - bol of
2. I have no wish to wield the sword of pow - er, I
3. Lord, let me love the low - ly and the hum - ble, for -

grace that warms my heart, of grace that warms my heart;
want no man to leap, to leap at my com - mand;
get - ting not the might - y, the might - y and the strong;

And let me find Thy lov - ing hand to still me, to
Nor let my crit - ics feel con-strained to cow - er,
And give me grace to love those who may stum - ble, to

still me when I trem - ble At Thy com-mand to love all
feel con-strained to cow - er For fear of some re - pri - sal
love those who may stum - ble, Nor let me seek to judge of

hu - man - kind.
at my hand.
right or wrong.

Lord, let me love, though love may be the
Lord, teach me mer - cy; let me be the
Lord, let my par - ish be the world un -

los - ing Of ev - 'ry earth - ly treas - ure I pos - sess.
win - ner Of ev - 'ry man's re - spect and sim - ple love.
bound - ed, Let love of race and clan be at an end.

Lord, make Thy love the pat - tern of my choos - ing.
For I have known Thy mer - cy, though a sin - ner,
Let ev - 'ry hate - ful doc - trine be con - found - ed

And let Thy will dic - tate my hap - pi - ness.
When - ev - er I have sought Thy peace a - bove.
That in - ter - dicts the love of friend for friend.

A - men.

A - men.   A - men.

Text: C. Eric Lincoln, 1924–2000, © 1958, Estate of C. Eric Lincoln
Tune: J. Jefferson Cleveland, 1937–1988, © 1981, Estate of J. Jefferson Cleveland

3   As a Fire Is Meant for Burning

1. As a fire is meant for burn-ing With a bright and warm-ing flame, So the church is meant for mis-sion, Giv - ing glo - ry to God's name. Not to preach our creeds or cus-toms, But to build a bridge of care, We join hands a -

2. We are learn - ers; we are teach - ers; We are pil - grims on the way. We are seek - ers; we are giv - ers; We are ves - sels made of clay. By our gen - tle, lov - ing ac - tions, We would show that Christ is light. In a hum - ble,

3. As a green bud in the spring-time Is a sign of life re - newed, So may we be signs of one - ness 'Mid earth's peo - ples, man - y hued. As a rain - bow lights the heav - ens When a storm is past and gone, May our lives re -

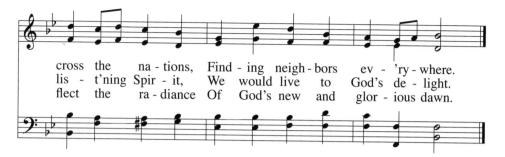

cross the na - tions, Find - ing neigh - bors ev - 'ry - where.
lis - t'ning Spir - it, We would live to God's de - light.
flect the ra - diance Of God's new and glor - ious dawn.

Text: Ruth Duck, b.1947, © 1992, GIA Publications, Inc.
Tune: BEECHER, 8 7 8 7 D; John Zundel, 1815–1882

4 As the Waters Rise around Us

1. As the wa-ters rise a-round us And the winds rage o-ver-head; As de-struc-tion's wake con-founds us With its mount-ing toll of dead: Lord, have mer-cy. Lord, have mer-cy. Lord, have

2. Numb with grief, our hearts are heav-y, Seek-ing cour-age to en-dure, As the harsh-est cost is lev-ied On the poor-est of the poor.

3. Homes and cit-y streets are rav-aged, Man-y lost be-yond re-pair. Brood-ing Spir-it, help us sal-vage Signs of life from such de-spair.

4. Gra-cious God, Your strong com-pas-sion Stilled the storm and part-ed seas. Free and lead us till we fash-ion Worlds of jus-tice, hope, and peace.

mer - cy. Hear your peo - ple's yearn - ing cry. Hear your peo - ple's yearn-ing cry.

Text: Mary Louise Bringle, b.1953, © 2006, GIA Publications, Inc.
Tune: BRYN CALFARIA, 8 7 8 7 with refrain; William Owen, 1814–1893

On August 29, 2005, Hurricane Katrina ravaged the Gulf Coast of the United States, destroying lives and livelihoods. Mary Louise Bringle wrote this text and sent it to the people of Central Presbyterian Church of Atlanta to use on the following Sunday, as they prepared to receive storm refugees.

5 Called to Gather as God's People

1. Called to gath - er as God's peo - ple, We as - sem - ble in this place To u - nite our hearts and voic - es In thanks - giv - ing for God's grace: For the birth - ing of cre - a - tion, For Christ's

2. Taught and formed by proc - la - ma - tion, We a - wait God's prom - ised word: Song and sto - ry, psalm and pre - cept, All the range of scrip - ture heard. By this an - cient, liv - ing wit - ness We are

3. Fed at Christ's a - bun - dant ta - ble, We par - take of ho - ly food, Wake the gifts of hope and mem - 'ry, Taste and see that God is good. So our min - gled lives are tak - en, Blessed and

4. Sent to share the Spir - it's bless - ing, We go forth re - newed, re - stored, Hum - bled by the task be - fore us, Strength - ened by the Love out - poured. Find - ing faith con - firmed in ac - tion, Led by

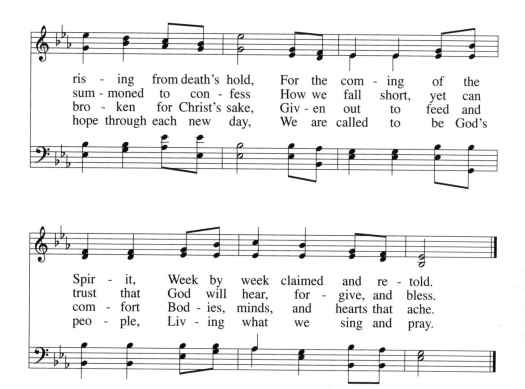

ris - ing from death's hold,   For the com - ing of the
sum - moned to con - fess   How we fall short, yet can
bro - ken for Christ's sake,   Giv - en out to feed and
hope through each new day,   We are called to be God's

Spir - it,   Week by week claimed and re - told.
trust that   God will hear, for - give, and bless.
com - fort   Bod - ies, minds, and hearts that ache.
peo - ple,   Liv - ing what we sing and pray.

Text: Carl P. Daw, Jr., b.1944, © 2001, Hope Publishing Co.
Tune: NETTLETON, 8 7 8 7 D; Wyeth's *Repository of Sacred Music, Pt. II,* 1813

1. Christ is a-live! Let Chris-tians sing.
2. Christ is a-live! No long-er bound
3. In ev-'ry in-sult, rift, and war,
4. Wom-en and men, in age and youth,
5. Christ is a-live, and comes to bring

The cross stands emp-ty to the sky.
To dis-tant years in Pal-es-tine,
Where col-or, scorn or wealth di-vide,
Can feel the Spir-it, hear the call,
Good news to this and ev-'ry age,

Let streets and homes with prais-es ring.
But sav-ing, heal-ing, here and now,
Christ suf-fers still, yet loves the more,
And find the way, the life, the truth,
Till earth and sky and o-cean ring

Love, drowned in death, shall nev-er die.
And touch-ing ev-'ry place and time.
And lives, where ev-en hope has died.
Re-vealed in Je-sus, freed for all.
With joy, with jus-tice, love and praise.

Text: Romans 6:5–11; Brian Wren, b.1936, © 1975, rev. 1995, Hope Publishing Co.
Tune: DUKE STREET, LM; John Hatton, c.1710–1793

1. Christ, we climb with You the mountain Where in sol - i -
2. Christ, stay with us on the moun-tain, For our hearts beat
3. Je - sus, send us to the val - ley Where the road through
4. Christ, trans - fig - ured on the moun-tain, Christ, who walked the

tude You pray. There Your gar - ments, white and glist - 'ning,
fast with fear While a might - y Voice that, thun - d'ring,
suf - f'ring leads. There we meet Your an - guished peo - ple;
earth to save! Christ, the Son of God in glo - ry,

Shine more bright - ly than the day. Face a - glow with
Brings God's maj - es - ty too near: "Know this man who
There Your world from vio - lence bleeds. Give us cour - age,
Christ, who took the form of slave! Help the church, Your

God's own glo - ry, You with an - cient proph - ets talk,
stands be - fore you Is the Christ, my Son, my own!
when we fal - ter, Not to shrink from pain or loss.
liv - ing Bod - y, Share with You Love's cost and pain;

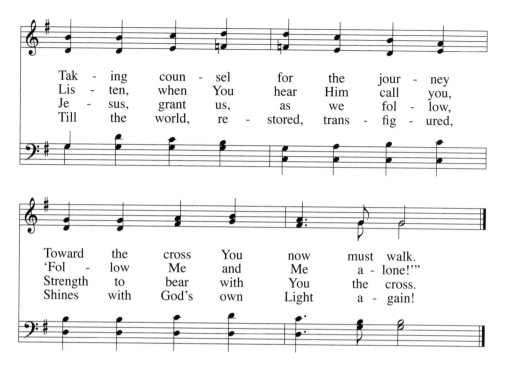

Tak - ing   coun - sel   for   the   jour - ney
Lis - ten,   when   You   hear   Him   call   you,
Je - sus,   grant   us,   as   we   fol - low,
Till   the   world,   re - stored,   trans - fig - ured,

Toward   the   cross   You   now   must   walk.
'Fol - low   Me   and   Me   a - lone!'"
Strength   to   bear   with   You   the   cross.
Shines   with   God's   own   Light   a - gain!

Text: Matthew 17:1–22, Mark 9:2–32, Luke 9:28–45; Herman G. Stuempfle, Jr., 1923–2007, © 2006, GIA Publications, Inc.
Tune: HYMN TO JOY, 8 7 8 7 D; arr. from Ludwig van Beethoven, 1770–1827, by Edward Hodges, 1796–1867

This page has been intentionally left blank.

Christ's Word to Us Is Like a Burning Fire   8

*Trumpets before each stanza
(optional)*

1. Christ's word to us is like a burn-ing
2. Where peo-ple long for free-dom, peace, and
3. When we are bowed by grief, de-feat, or
4. So shall the Word, still like a burn-ing

fire, Sear - ing our hearts, our ac - tions to in-
bread, But they are giv - en chains and strife in-
fear, Warm and ig - nite the fire of faith and
fire, Be all the truth and wis - dom we re-

spire. Burn deep with - in, O Christ, for - give and
stead, Grant us the flame of cour - age, light of
cheer. So may we be em-pow'red to do the
quire, Flash - ing new in - sight, mak - ing vi - sion

cleanse. Show us the world through God's own per - fect lens.
truth. Use us, O God, now with the strength of youth.
right, Liv - ing from dark - ness in - to dawn-ing light.
clear, Re - veal-ing Christ a - mong us now and here.

Text: Jane Parker Huber, © 1986, admin. by Westminster John Knox Press
Tune: NATIONAL HYMN, 10 10 10 10; George W. Warren, 1828–1902

Clear the cha - os and the clut - ter,
Mak - ing space with - in our think - ing,
There's a place for deep - est dream - ing,

Clear our eyes, that we can see
Lift - ing shades to show the sun,
There's a time for heart to care,

All the things that real - ly mat - ter,
Rais - ing cour - age when we're shrink - ing,
In the Spir - it's live - ly schem - ing

Be at peace, and sim - ply be.
Find - ing scope for faith be - gun.
There is al - ways room to spare!

Text: Shirley Erena Murray, b.1931, © 1992, Hope Publishing Co.
Tune: CONVERSE, 8 7 8 7 D; Charles C. Converse, 1832–1918

10 Come, Let Us Praise What God Has Done

1. Come, let us praise what God has done, And all that God will do, Whose love is old-er than the sun, And yet for-ev-er new.

2. When slaves in E-gypt, long a-go, Were plead-ing to be free, God said, through Mo-ses, "Let them go!", And led them through the sea.

3. Re-mem-ber-ing that old sur-prise, In ex-ile and de-spair, The proph-ets cried, "A-wake! A-rise! The way of God pre-pare!"

4. God's free-ing love a-gain was shown: By pa-gan king's de-cree The peo-ple came re-joic-ing home, For all the world to see.

5. And what of Christ, who rose from death When life and hope were lost, And gave us, by the Spir-it's breath, The pow'r of Pen-te-cost?

6. Through man-y years, and still to-day, Christ, end-less-ly a-live, Has trav-eled with us on our way, And waits where we ar-rive.

7. Let ev-'ry-thing that God has done Our faith and hope re-new To love and hon-or ev-'ry-one And show what God can do.

Text: Brian Wren, b.1936, © 1996, Hope Publishing Co.
Tune: AZMON, CM; Carl G. Gläser, 1784–1829; harm. by Lowell Mason, 1792–1872

1. Hear the bless - ed Sav - ior call - ing the op - pressed,
2. Are you dis - ap - point - ed, wan - d'ring here and there,
3. Stum - bling on the moun - tains dark with sin and shame,
4. Have you cares of bus - 'ness, cares of press - ing debt?
5. Have you by temp - ta - tion of - ten con - quered been,

"O ye heav - y - lad - en, come to Me and rest;
Drag - ging chains of doubt and load - ed down with care?
Stum - bling toward the pit of hell's con - sum - ing flame;
Cares of so - cial life or cares of hopes un - met?
Has a sense of weak - ness brought dis - tress with - in?

Come, no long - er tar - ry, I your load will bear,
Do un - ho - ly feel - ings strug - gle in your breast?
By the pow'rs of sin de - lud - ed and op - pressed,
Are you by re - morse or sense of guilt de - pressed?
Christ will sanc - ti - fy you, if you'll claim His best,

Bring Me ev - 'ry bur - den, bring Me ev - 'ry care."
Bring your case to Je - sus, He will give you rest.
Hear the ten - der Shep - herd, "Come to Me and rest."
Come right on to Je - sus, He will give you rest.
In the Ho - ly Spir - it He will give you rest.

Come and trust My might;

Come and trust My might,

Come and trust my might;

Come,

Come, O come,

My yoke is eas - y,

Come, My yoke is eas - y,

And

light.

My bur - den's Come, My bur - den's light.

Come, O come,

Come, My bur - den's light.

Text: Charles P. Jones, 1865–1949
Tune: COME UNTO ME, 11 11 11 11 with refrain; Charles P. Jones, 1865–1949

12 Count It All Joy

I count ev-'ry-thing as joy in Christ Je-sus. I count
ev-'ry-thing as joy in the Lord. All the
vic - t'ries I share, all the bur - dens I bear,
ev-'ry-thing, ev-'ry-thing, ev-'ry-thing in Christ is joy.

If you're sick, He's a doc-tor, that's joy. If in
trou-ble, He's a law-yer, that's joy. What-
ev-er the prob-lem, He can solve them. Ev-'ry-thing,
ev-'ry-thing, ev-'ry-thing in Christ is joy.

Text: Margaret Pleasant Douroux, b.1941
Tune: Margaret Pleasant Douroux, b.1941
© Rev. Earl Pleasant Publishing Co.

13   Faith Begins by Letting Go

1. Faith be-
2. Faith en-
3. Faith ma-

gins by let-ting go, Giv-ing up what had seemed
dures by hold-ing on, Keep-ing mem-'ry's roots a-
tures by reach-ing out, Stretch-ing minds, en-larg-ing

sure, Tak-ing risks and press-ing on, Though the
live So that hope may bear its fruit; Prom-ise-
hearts, Shar-ing strug-gles, liv-ing prayer, Bind-ing

way   feels less se - cure: Pil - grim - age both right and
fed,   our souls will thrive,   Not through mer - it we pos-
up   the bro - ken parts: Till we find the com - mon-

odd,   Trust - ing all our life to God.
sess   But by God's great faith - ful - ness.
place   Ripe with wit - ness to God's grace.

Coda

Text: Carl P. Daw, Jr., b.1944, © 1996, Hope Publishing Co.
Tune: JULION, 7 7 7 7 7 7; David Hurd, b.1950, © 1983, GIA Publications, Inc.

14 Follow Jesus

♩ = 58

1. Fol - low Je - sus, take no chance get - ting lost. Fol-low
2. Fol - low Je - sus, He will lead, He will guide. Fol-low

Je - sus, There'll be des - erts you'll have to cross. Fol - low Je -
Je - sus, Through life's tem - pest He'll let you hide. Fol - low Je -

sus. He's got a safe moun - tain plan; and if
sus. Reach out and touch, hold His hand;

He can't take you to the top, there's no-bod-y else who can.

Don't wor-ry if you can-not see, learn to trust Him and to fol-low His lead. Don't wor-ry if it's day or night. He is bright-er than the bright-est light. And if He can't take you to the top, there's no-bod-y else who can.

Last time

Text: Margaret Pleasant Douroux, b.1941, © 1981, Rev. Earl Pleasant Publishing Co.
Tune: Margaret Pleasant Douroux, b.1941, © 1981, Rev. Earl Pleasant Publishing Co.; arr. by Kenneth W. Louis, b.1956, © 2006, GIA Publications, Inc.

15 For the Healing of the Nations

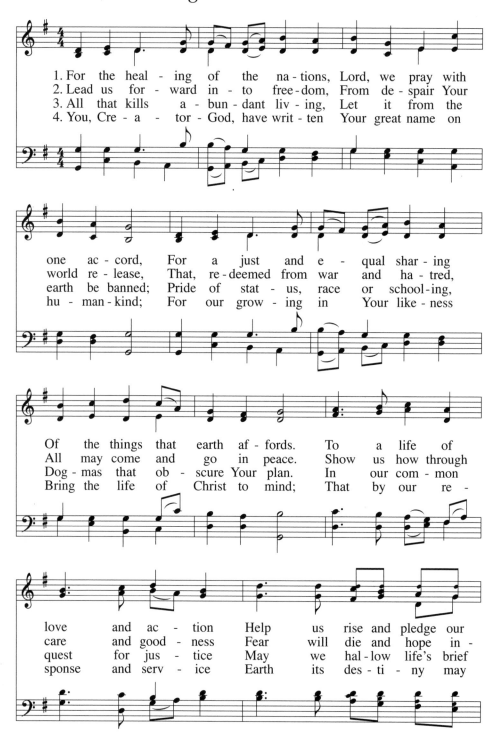

1. For the heal - ing of the na - tions, Lord, we pray with
2. Lead us for - ward in - to free - dom, From de - spair Your
3. All that kills a - bun - dant liv - ing, Let it from the
4. You, Cre - a - tor - God, have writ - ten Your great name on

one ac - cord, For a just and e - qual shar - ing
world re - lease, That, re - deemed from war and ha - tred,
earth be banned; Pride of stat - us, race or school-ing,
hu - man-kind; For our grow - ing in Your like - ness

Of the things that earth af - fords. To a life of
All may come and go in peace. Show us how through
Dog - mas that ob - scure Your plan. In our com - mon
Bring the life of Christ to mind; That by our re -

love and ac - tion Help us rise and pledge our
care and good - ness Fear will die and hope in -
quest for jus - tice May we hal - low life's brief
sponse and serv - ice Earth its des - ti - ny may

word.
crease.
span.
find.

Help us rise and pledge our word.
Fear will die and hope in - crease.
May we hal - low life's brief span.
Earth its des - ti - ny may find.

Text: Fred Kaan, b.1929, alt. © 1968, Hope Publishing Co.
Tune: CWM RHONDDA, 8 7 8 7 8 77; John Hughes, 1873–1932

16 For the Music of Creation

1. For the mu-sic of cre-a-tion, For the song Your
Spir-it sings, For Your sound's di-vine ex-pres-sion,
Burst of joy in liv-ing things: God, our God, the
world's com-pos-er, Hear us, ech-oes of Your voice—

2. Psalms and sym-pho-nies ex-alt You, Drum and trum-pet,
string and reed, Sim-ple mel-o-dies ac-claim You,
Tunes that rise from deep-est need, Hymns of long-ing
and be-long-ing, Car-ols from a cheer-ful throat,

3. All the voic-es of the a-ges In tran-scen-dent
cho-rus meet, Wor-ship lift-ing up the sens-es,
Hands that praise, and danc-ing feet; O-ver dis-cord
and di-vi-sion Mu-sic speaks Your joy and peace,

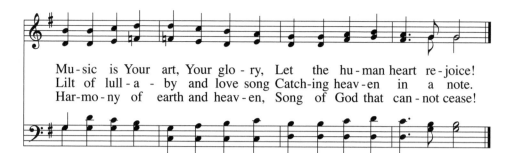

Mu-sic is Your art, Your glo-ry, Let the hu-man heart re-joice!
Lilt of lull-a - by and love song Catch-ing heav-en in a note.
Har-mo-ny of earth and heav-en, Song of God that can-not cease!

Text: Shirley Erena Murray, b.1931, © 1992, Hope Publishing Co.
Tune: HYMN TO JOY, 8 7 8 7 D; arr. from Ludwig van Beethoven, 1770–1827, by Edward Hodges, 1796–1867

17 Glorify His Name

1. Praise Him, praise Him, all ye na - tions,
2. Let us do the things He bids us,
3. Though at times He seems not near us,
4. When our Sav - ior in His glo - ry,

All His won - drous love pro - claim, Sing with rap - ture
Let the world de - ride or blame, We shall con - quer
And the world would us be - shame, Yet, O saints, through
Comes His bless - ed ones to claim, We shall meet Him

of His bless - ings, Sing and glo - ri - fy His name!
if we ev - er Live to glo - ri - fy His name!
all the dark - ness, Live to glo - ri - fy His name!
and be with Him, There to glo - ri - fy His name!

Sing to glo - ri - fy His name, Sing to

Sing to glo - ri - fy His name, Sing to glo - ri - fy His name, Sing to

glo - ri - fy His name;

glo - ri - fy His name, Sing to glo - ri - fy His name.

All ye ran-somed chil-dren, ev - er Glo - ri - fy the Sav-ior's name.

Text: Amelia Gaynor Anderson
Tune: Charles P. Jones, 1865–1949

18   Go to the World!

as the sign of our re - birth.
pres - ence in each time and space.
Church, you fol - low Christ's own way. Al -
hosts of glo - ry cry "A - men!"

le - lu - ia. Al - le - lu - ia.

Text: Sylvia G. Dunstan, 1955–1993, © 1991, GIA Publications, Inc.
Tune: SINE NOMINE, 10 10 10 with alleluias; Ralph Vaughan Williams, 1872–1958

19 God Has Not Said

1. God has not said, you shall be free From per-
2. Through Christ, the Son, our cour-teous Lord, Who cost-
3. Christ stands in strength a - gainst all pow'rs. His force
4. We bow, O Christ, be - fore Your cross: Your death,
5. By Love, for Love, in Love most pure The will

il and from pain. But you who trust My stead - fast
ly death en - dured, Our price is paid with right - eous
is self - less grace. In this a - lone His church can
our ran - somed life. You show our hearts the path to
of God shines clear. All shall be well! Our com - fort

heart Shall not be tried in vain!
blood, Our place in heav'n pro - cured.
boast: Our Lord, whose shield is peace.
joy In faith - ful sac - ri - fice.
sure: The ris - en Christ is here!

Text: Mary Louise Bringle, b.1953, © 2006, GIA Publications, Inc.
Tune: MARTYRDOM, CM; Hugh Wilson, 1766-1824; arr. by Nolan Williams, Jr., b.1969, © 2000, GIA Publications, Inc.

1. God of free-dom, God of jus-tice, You whose love is
2. Rid the earth of tor-ture's ter-ror, You whose hands were
3. Make in us a cap-tive con-science Quick to hear, to

strong as death, You who saw the dark of pris-on,
nailed to wood; Hear the cries of pain and pro-test,
act, to plead; Make us tru-ly sis-ters, broth-ers

You who knew the price of faith— Touch our world of
You who shed the tears and blood— Move in us the
Of what-ev-er race or creed— Teach us to be

sad op-pres-sion With Your Spir-it's heal-ing breath.
pow'r of pit-y Rest-less for the com-mon good.
ful-ly hu-man, O-pen to each oth-er's needs.

Text: Shirley Erena Murray, b.1931, © 1992, Hope Publishing Co.
Tune: REGENT SQUARE, 8 7 8 7 8 7; Henry Smart, 1813–1879

21 God of Futures Yet Unfolding

1. God of fu - tures yet un - fold - ing, Ev - er mak - ing all things
2. God of ev - 'ry fresh cre - a - tion, Tend us with a gar-d'ner's
3. God of res - ur - rec-tion splen-dor, Burn a - way the haze of

new: Grant us path - ways in our wan - d'ring, Light when
hand. On Your peo - ple pour Your Spir - it, Wa - ter
fear. Clear our hearts to face to - mor - row Bright with

dark - ness dims our view. O - pen doors when dread de - feats us.
on a thirst - y land: Till we spring like grass - y mead-ows,
hope's un - fad - ing cheer. Through the fu - ture's vast un - fold - ing,

Set dis - cour - aged cap-tives free. God of fu - tures yet un -
Pop-lar trees by flow - ing streams. God of ev - 'ry fresh cre -
In each new cre - a - tion's breath, God of res - ur - rec-tion

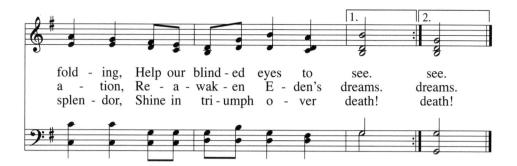

fold - ing, Help our blind - ed eyes to see. see.
a - tion, Re - a - wak - en E - den's dreams. dreams.
splen - dor, Shine in tri - umph o - ver death! death!

Text: Mary Louise Bringle, b.1953, © 2002, GIA Publications, Inc.
Tune: ALL THE WAY, 8 7 8 7 D; Robert Lowry, 1826-1899

22 God of History—Recent, Ancient

1. God of his - t'ry— re - cent, an - cient—
2. You have called us from di - vi - sion
3. How are we, then, called to an - swer
4. God, You point us toward the fu - ture

God of ev - 'ry yes - ter - day,
In - to u - ni - ty and hope.
As we work and as we live,
Where Christ leads and shows the way.

Still our God in this day's mo - ments,
Each and all be - long to - geth - er
Called to jus - tice, called to mis - sion,
Here and now, work not yet fin - ished

Where we go or where we stay:
In the world's ka - lei - do - scope.
Learn - ing to re - ceive and give?
Needs our strength and will to - day.

You have set us in this con - text,
Help us lis - ten to the voic - es
Shall we build a bridge of prom - ise?
Thus we move in - to to - mor - row,

Time, re - la - tion - ship, and place,
Dar - ing us to be and do
Tear down walls that split, di - vide?
Called to live and work and be

Hear our praise and glad thanks - giv - ing
What You plan for church and peo - ple,
Fling wide door - ways, o - pen win - dows?
Rec - on - cil - ers, pil - grim peo - ple,

For all signs of pre - sent grace.
Lov - ing oth - ers, prais - ing You.
Let the Spir - it come in - side?
Called by Christ, by Christ set free.

Text: Jane Parker Huber, b.1926, © 1984, admin. by Westminster John Knox Press
Tune: HYFRYDOL, 8 7 8 7 D; Rowland H. Prichard, 1811–1887

23 God of Wisdom, Truth, and Beauty

1. God of wis-dom, truth, and beau-ty, God of spir-it,
2. God of dra-ma, mu-sic, danc-ing, God of sto-ry,
3. God of at-om's small-est fea-ture, God of gal-ax-
4. God of sci-ence, his-t'ry, teach-ing, God of fu-tures

fire, and soul, God of or-der, love, and du-ty,
sculp-ture, art, God of wit, all life en-hanc-ing,
ies in space, God of ev-'ry liv-ing crea-ture,
yet un-known, God of hold-ing, God of reach-ing,

God of pur-pose, plan, and goal: Grant us vi-sions ev-er
God of ev-'ry yearn-ing heart: Chal-lenge us with quests of
God of all the hu-man race: May our knowl-edge be ex-
God of pow'r be-yond each throne: Take the frag-ments of our

grow-ing, Breath of life, e-ter-nal strength, Mys-tic spir-it,
spir-it, Truth re-vealed in myr-iad ways, Word or song for
tend-ed For the whole cre-a-tion's good, Hun-ger ban-ished,
liv-ing. Fit us to Your fin-est scheme. Now for-giv-en

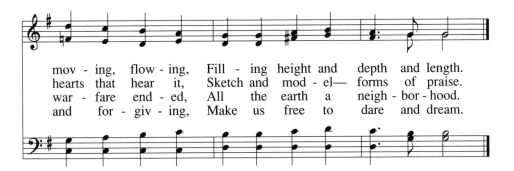

mov - ing, flow - ing, Fill - ing height and depth and length.
hearts that hear it, Sketch and mod - el— forms of praise.
war - fare end - ed, All the earth a neigh - bor - hood.
and for - giv - ing, Make us free to dare and dream.

Text: Jane Parker Huber, b.1926, © 1984, admin. by Westminster John Knox Press
Tune: HYMN TO JOY, 8 7 8 7 D; arr. from Ludwig van Beethoven, 1770–1827, by Edward Hodges, 1796–1867

24   Gracious Spirit, Give Your Servants

1. Gra - cious Spir - it, give Your ser - vants
2. Word made flesh, who gave up glo - ry
3. Lov - ing God who birthed cre - a - tion
4. Tri - une God, e - ter - nal Be - ing,

Joy to set sin's cap - tives free,
To be - come our great high priest,
From the noth - ing - ness of space,
Nev - er - end - ing, un - be - gun,

Hope to heal the bro - ken - heart - ed,
Tak - ing on our hu - man na - ture
Kin - dling life where all was emp - ty,
Bound - less grace and per - fect jus - tice,

Peace to share love's lib - er - ty.
To re - deem the last and least:
Turn - ing cha - os in - to grace:
Right - eous and for - giv - ing One:

Through us bring Your balm of glad - ness
Let Your cour - age and com - pas - sion
When we feel con - fused and fruit - less,
So en - fold us in Your mer - cy

To the wound - ed and op - pressed;
Shape and guide our min - is - tries;
Dawn up - on our rest - less night;
That our wills and Yours u - nite;

Help us claim and show God's fa - vor
As our Sav - ior and our Shep - herd,
Give us faith's i - mag - i - na - tion,
Through us may the world be - hold You,

As a peo - ple called and blessed.
Lead us to the truth that frees.
Hope's re - new - ing, love's de - light.
Find Your love, Your truth, Your light.

Text: Carl P. Daw, Jr., b.1944, © 1997, Hope Publishing Co.
Tune: HYFRYDOL, 8 7 8 7 D; Rowland H. Prichard, 1811–1887

25 Great Spirit, Joy of Earth and Sky

1. Great Spir - it, joy of earth and sky, We
2. Re - main be - side us, ho - ly friend; Sus -
3. High rug - ged cliffs, wide rush - ing streams, O
4. In times of laugh - ter, times of tears, When
5. A - mong us all who gath - er here May

seek Your pres - ence now, That two may join
tain us by Your pow'r, That we may keep
Spir - it, guide us past, With grow - ing love
hopes are lost and born, Give us the strength
jus - tice, love in - crease. Cre - ate with - in

in cov - e - nant And free - ly make their vow.
in faith and hope Com - mit - ments made this hour.
as years go by, The best joy saved till last.
and gen - tle - ness To build, to dance, to mourn.
us ten - der hearts And fill our lives with peace.

Text: Ecclesiastes 3:1–8, Ruth Duck, b.1947, © 1992, GIA Publications, Inc.
Tune: NEW BRITAIN, CM; *Virginia Harmony*, 1831; harm. by Edwin O. Excell, 1851–1921

1. Help us ac-cept each oth-er As Christ ac-cept-ed us;
2. Teach us, O Lord, Your les-sons, As in our dai-ly life
3. Let Your ac-cept-ance change us, So that we may be moved
4. Lord, for to-day's en-coun-ters With all who are in need,

Teach us as sis-ter, broth-er, Each per-son to em-brace.
We strug-gle to be hu-man And search for hope and faith.
In liv-ing sit-u-a-tions To do the truth in love;
Who hun-ger for ac-cept-ance, For right-eous-ness and bread,

Be pres-ent, Lord, a-mong us, And bring us to be-lieve
Teach us to care for peo-ple, For all, not just for some;
To prac-tice Your ac-cept-ance, Un-til we know by heart
We need new eyes for see-ing, New hands for hold-ing on;

We are our-selves ac-cept-ed And meant to love and live.
To love them as we find them, Or as they may be-come.
The ta-ble of for-give-ness And laugh-ter's heal-ing art.
Re-new us with Your Spir-it; Lord, free us, make us one!

Text: Romans 15:7; Fred Kaan, b.1929, © 1975, Hope Publishing Co.
Tune: AURELIA, 7 6 7 6 D; Samuel Sebastian Wesley, 1810–1876

27 Help Us Forgive, Forgiving Lord

1. Help us for-give, for-giv-ing Lord, The
2. For on the cross You bore for us The
3. Let grace un-lock each pris-oned heart, Un -
4. And then, the bro-ken cir-cle closed, The

wrong that oth-ers do And, when our hearts are
curse, the scorn, the hate And gave Your life to
coil each fist-ed hand Un-til from hate our
bro-ken friend-ships healed, Lord, hold us fast with -

pierced by pain, To bring the hurt to You.
lift from us Sin's cruel and crush-ing weight.
hearts are freed, Our hands in love ex-tend.
in the bonds By Your for-give-ness sealed.

Text: Matthew 18:21–35, Romans 12:9–21; Herman G. Stuempfle, Jr., 1923–2007, © 1997, GIA Publications, Inc.
Tune: ARLINGTON, CM; Thomas A. Arne, 1710–1778

1. How great the mys - ter - y of faith,
2. At - tract - ed by life's deep - est claim
3. The best that we can do and say,
4. Come, walk a - mong us, Ho - ly Friend,

How deep the pur - pos - es of God,
We wait, as - sem - bled in this place,
The ut - most care of skill and art,
As all are gath - ered and pre - pared,

In birth and age - ing, life and death,
With needs and hopes we can - not name,
Are sweep - ers of the Spir - it's way
That scat - tered lives may meet and mend

Un - veiled, yet nev - er un - der - stood!
A - thirst for heal - ing, truth and grace.
To reach the depths of ev - 'ry heart.
Through o - pen Word and ta - ble shared.

Text: Brian Wren, b.1936, © 1989, Hope Publishing Co.
Tune: WOODWORTH, LM; John Hatton, c. 1710–1793

29 How Long, O Lord, How Long?

1. "How long, O Lord, how long," The starv-ing mil-lions cry, "Shall fam-ine's blight our lives de-stroy, Our chil-dren waste and die?"
2. How long, O Lord, how long Must home-less peo-ple lie With-out a bed in street and camp While oth-ers pass them by?
3. How long, O Lord, how long Will jus-tice bow to greed, And wealth and pow-er forge the chains That hold the poor in need?
4. How long, O Lord, how long Will walls we build di-vide, And pride of gen-der, race or class An-oth-er's worth de-ride?
5. How long, O Lord, how long Must war its car-nage spread, And leave be-hind in ru-ined rows The har-vest of the dead?
6. "How long, O Lord, how long?" We cry in our de-spair; Yet, nailed up-on the cross we see The em-blem of Your care.
7. How long, O Lord, how long? Grant strength of heart and nerve To share Your work of truth and love, To suf-fer and to serve.
8. How long, O Lord, how long Will e-vil's pow'r pre-vail? We hope in Christ who con-quered death, Whose pur-pose can-not fail.

Text: Herman G. Stuempfle, Jr., 1923–2007, © 1993, GIA Publications, Inc.
Tune: TRENTHAM, SM; Robert Jackson, 1840–1914

1. How wonderful the Three-in-One,
Whose energies of dancing light
Are undivided, pure and good,
Communing love in shared delight.

2. Before the flow of dawn and dark,
Creation's Lover dreamed of earth,
And with a caring deep and wise,
All things conceived and brought to birth.

3. The Lover's own Belov'd, in time,
Between a cradle and a cross,
At home in flesh, gave love and life,
To heal our brokenness and loss.

4. Their Equal Friend all life sustains
With greening pow'r and loving care,
And calls us, born again by grace,
In Love's communing life to share.

5. How wonderful the Living God:
Divine Belov'd Empow'ring Friend,
Eternal Lover, Three-in-One,
Our hope's beginning, way and end.

Text: Brian Wren, b.1936, © 1989, Hope Publishing Co.
Tune: OLD HUNDREDTH, LM; Louis Bourgeois, c.1510–1561

31 I Am Kept by the Grace of God

I am kept by the grace of God. I am kept by the grace, the grace of God. He pro- tects me, He dir - ects me. Keeps a hedge all a- round me. I'm kept by the grace of God.

Text: Jimmy Dowell
Tune: Jimmy Dowell; arr. by James Abbington
© 1993, Jimmy Dowell

I Come with Joy   32

1. I come with joy, a child of God, For - giv - en,
2. I come with Chris - tians far and near To find, as
3. As Christ breaks bread, and bids us share, Each proud di -
4. The Spir - it of the ris - en Christ, Un - seen, but
5. To - geth - er met, to - geth - er bound By all that

loved, and free, The life of Je - sus to re - call, In
all are fed, The new com - mu - ni - ty of love In
vi - sion ends. The love that made us, makes us one, And
ev - er near, Is in such friend-ship bet - ter known, A -
God has done, We'll go with joy, to give the world The

love laid down for me. The life of Je - sus
Christ's com - mu - nion bread. The new com - mu - ni -
stran - gers now are friends. The love that made us,
live a - mong us here. Is in such friend - ship
love that makes us one. We'll go with joy, to

to re - call, In love laid down for me.
ty of love In Christ's com - mu - nion bread.
makes us one, And stran - gers now are friends.
bet - ter known, A - live a - mong us here.
give the world The love that makes us one.

Text: Brian Wren, b.1936, © 1971, 1995, Hope Publishing Co.
Tune: CORONATION, CM with repeat; Oliver Holden, 1765–1844

33 I Was Glad When They Said unto Me

seek Thy good and praise Thy ho - ly name.

I will praise Thy name, praise Thy name,

praise Thy ho - ly name. In the house of the Lord will I

seek Thy good and praise Thy ho - ly name.

name. I will praise Thy ho - ly name.

cresc. and rit.

Text: Psalm 122; Laymon T. Hunter
Tune: Laymon T. Hunter
© 1965, 1973, Laymon T. Hunter

34 In an Age of Twisted Values

1. In an age of twist - ed val - ues
2. We have built dis - crim - i - na - tion
3. When our fam - i - lies are bro - ken,
4. We who hear Your word so of - ten

We have lost the truth we need.
On our prej - u - dice and fear.
When our homes are full of strife,
Choose so rare - ly to o - bey.

In so - phis - ti - ca - ted lan - guage
Ha - tred swift - ly turns to cruel - ty
When our chil - dren are be - wil - dered,
Turn us from our will - ful blind - ness;

We have jus - ti - fied our greed.
If we hold re - sent - ments dear.
When they lose their way in life,
Give us truth to light our way.

By our strug - gle for pos - ses - sions
For com - mu - ni - ties di - vid - ed
When we fail to give the a - ged
In the pow - er of Your Spir - it

We have robbed the poor and weak.
By the walls of class and race,
All the care we know they need,
Come to cleanse us, make us new;

Hear our cry and heal our na - tion;
Hear our cry and heal our na - tion;
Hear our cry and heal our na - tion;
Hear our cry and heal our na - tion

Your for - give - ness, Lord, we seek.
Show us, Lord, Your love and grace.
Help us show more love, we plead.
Till our na - tion hon - ors You.

Text: Martin E. Leckebusch, b.1962, © 2000, Kevin Mayhew Ltd.
Tune: EBENEZER, 8 7 8 7 D; Thomas J. Williams, 1869–1944

35 In the Name of Christ We Gather

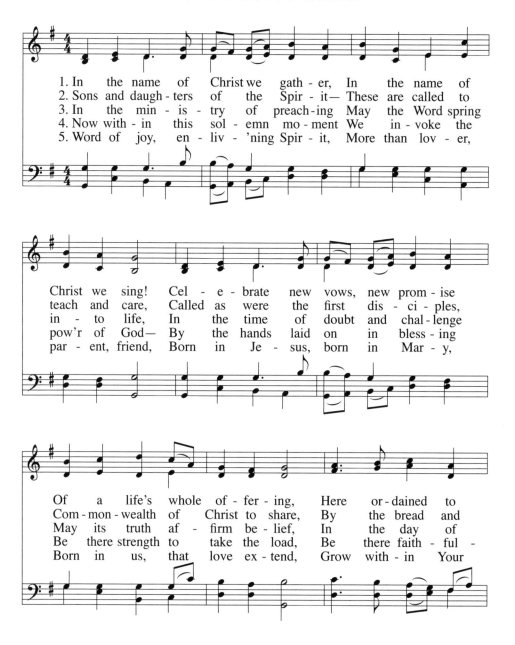

1. In the name of Christ we gath - er, In the name of
2. Sons and daugh - ters of the Spir - it— These are called to
3. In the min - is - try of preach-ing May the Word spring
4. Now with - in this sol - emn mo - ment We in - voke the
5. Word of joy, en - liv - 'ning Spir - it, More than lov - er,

Christ we sing! Cel - e - brate new vows, new prom - ise
teach and care, Called as were the first dis - ci - ples,
in - to life, In the time of doubt and chal - lenge
pow'r of God— By the hands laid on in bless - ing
par - ent, friend, Born in Je - sus, born in Mar - y,

Of a life's whole of - fer - ing, Here or - dained to
Com - mon - wealth of Christ to share, By the bread and
May its truth af - firm be - lief, In the day of
Be there strength to take the load, Be there faith - ful -
Born in us, that love ex - tend, Grow with - in Your

lead	God's	peo	-	ple	At	the	Gos -	pel's	beck	- on -
wine	and	wa	-	ter	Sac	-	ra - ments	of	grace	de -
pain	and	dark	-	ness	Heal	the	hurt	of	guilt	and
ness	in	lov	-	ing,	Be	there	cour -	age	for	this
cho	- sen	ser	-	vant,	Life	of	God	that	has	no

ing,	At	the	Gos -	pel's	beck -	on -	ing.
clare,	Sac	-	ra - ments	of	grace	de -	clare.
grief,	Heal	the	hurt	of	guilt	and	grief.
road,	Be	there	cour -	age	for	this	road.
end,	Life	of	God	that	has	no	end!

Text: Shirley Erena Murray, b.1931, © 1992, Hope Publishing Co.
Tune: CWM RHONDDA, 8 7 8 7 8 77; John Hughes, 1873–1932

36 Jesus Only

1. "Je - sus on - ly" is my mot - to, "Je - sus on - ly"
2. Je - sus on - ly shall com - mand me, Je - sus on - ly
3. Je - sus on - ly is my Cap - tain, He shall lead me
4. Then a - way with ev - 'ry i - dol, Let my Lord be

is my song, "Je - sus on - ly" is my heart - thought,
guide my way; On - ly He to choose my chang - es,
forth to fight; Je - sus on - ly is my ar - mor,
all to me; Je - sus on - ly is my Mas - ter,

"Je - sus on - ly" all day long.
None but Je - sus ev - 'ry day.
Je - sus on - ly is my might. None but Je - sus,
Je - sus on - ly let me see.

Sav - ior, Cap - tain, None but Je - sus help me sing;

Fill me ev - er with Thy pres - ence, Je - sus, Je - sus, Lord and King.

Text: Charles P. Jones, 1865–1949
Tune: JESUS ONLY, 8 7 8 7 with refrain; Charles P. Jones, 1865–1949

1. Lead on, O cloud of Pres - ence; The ex - o - dus is come;
2. Lead on, O fier - y pil - lar; We fol - low yet with fears,
3. Lead on, O God of free - dom, And guide us on our way,

In wil - der - ness and des - ert Our tribe shall make its home.
But we shall come re - joic - ing, Though joy be born of tears.
And help us trust the prom - ise Through strug - gle and de - lay.

Our bond-age left be - hind us, New hopes with - in us grow.
We are not lost, though wand - 'ring, For by Your light we come,
We pray our sons and daugh - ters May jour - ney to that land

We seek the land of prom - ise Where milk and hon - ey flow.
And we are still God's peo - ple. The jour - ney is our home.
Where jus - tice dwells with mer - cy And love is law's de - mand.

Text: Ruth Duck, b.1947, © 1992, GIA Publications, Inc.
Tune: LANCASHIRE, 7 6 7 6 D; Henry T. Smart, 1813–1879

38 Living Stones

1. Liv - ing stones, we raise a tem - ple Where the
2. Made of mar - ble, brick, or tim - ber, And the
3. Formed in faith, we join to - geth - er At the

Spir - it comes to dwell In each act of
la - bor of our hands, May our build - ings
ta - ble of our Lord. When we share in

lov - ing serv - ice, In the gos - pel truth we
house a peo - ple Who em - bod - y God's com -
cel - e - bra - tion, We de - part with strength re -

tell. In the plac - es where we wor - ship,
mands: In a world where home - less mil - lions
stored: To cre - ate a realm of jus - tice

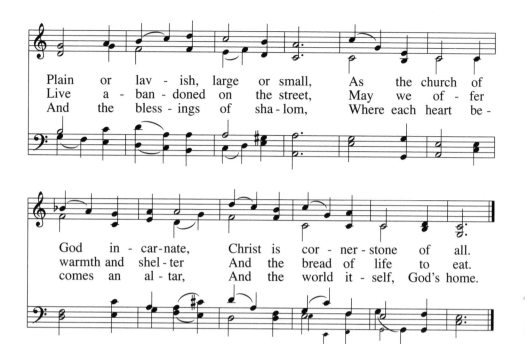

Plain or lav - ish, large or small, As the church of
Live a - ban - doned on the street, May we of - fer
And the bless - ings of sha - lom, Where each heart be -

God in - car - nate, Christ is cor - ner - stone of all.
warmth and shel - ter And the bread of life to eat.
comes an al - tar, And the world it - self, God's home.

Text: Mary Louise Bringle, b.1953, © 2006, GIA Publications, Inc.
Tune: ABBOT'S LEIGH, 8 7 8 7 D; Cyril V. Taylor, 1907–1991, © 1942, 1970, Hope Publishing Co.

This page has been intentionally left blank.

Lord, Help Us Walk Your Servant Way   39

1. Lord, help us walk Your ser-vant way Wher-ev-er love may lead And, bend-ing low, for-get-ting self, Each serve the oth-er's need.

2. You came to earth, O Christ, as Lord, But pow'r You laid a-side. You lived Your years in ser-vant-hood, In low-li-ness You died.

3. No gold-en scep-ter but a towel You place with-in the hands Of those who seek to fol-low You And live by Your com-mands.

4. You bid us bend our hu-man pride Nor count our-selves a-bove The low-est place, the mean-est task That waits the gift of love.

5. Lord, help us walk Your ser-vant way Wher-ev-er love may lead And bend-ing low, for-get-ting self, Each serve the oth-er's need.

Text: Mark 10:35–45, John 13:1–7, 31b–35; Herman G. Stuempfle, Jr., 1923–2007, © 1997, GIA Publications, Inc.
Tune: McKEE, CM; African-American; adapt. by Harry T. Burleigh, 1866–1949

40 Love One Another

1. It was love that brought the Sav - ior from on high,
2. We should love our Sav - ior and His word o - bey,
3. Let us tell of Je - sus and His pow'r to save,

It was love that caused Him here to bleed and die,
We should love to walk with - in the nar - row way,
Of the price - less bless - ings to the world He gave,

It was love that raised us from that aw - ful fall,
For the love of God will make us bold to win
How He calls the "who - so - ev - er" to His fold

It was love that heard our ur - gent call.
Pre - cious vic - t'ries o'er the world of sin.
Through the love that nev - er can be told.

oth - er,

We must love one an-oth-er, we must love one an-oth-er, And

thus ful-fill the roy-al law of God; We must love one an -

oth - er,

oth - er, we must love one an-oth-er, And thus ful-fill God's law.

oth - er,

Text: John 15:12; Romans 13:8; Gladstone T. Haywood, 1880–1931
Tune: LOVE ONE ANOTHER, 11 11 11 9 with refrain; Gladstone T. Haywood, 1880–1931

41 Mighty God Who Called Creation

1. Might-y God who called cre - a - tion From the un - formed womb of space, New - born worlds of gleam-ing glo - ry, Fresh with hope and ripe with grace: Speak a - gain with pow'r and prom - ise When the

2. As we wor - ship, may Your Spir - it Breathe through us the pow'r of prayer, Words of life for dai - ly liv - ing, Strength to do and faith to dare. Come, en - flame us, Ho - ly Spir - it, Like the

3. Root - ed in the love of Je - sus, Nour - ished by His flesh and blood, May we prove a fruit - ful vine - yard Joined in mu - tual ser - vant - hood. Work through us, O ris - en Sav - ior, To reap

4. Keep us faith - ful, joy - ful, lov - ing, Filled with hope through grief and pain, Know-ing that the One who made us Has re - deemed and will sus - tain: Tri - une God, of bound-less glo - ry, Yet in

storms of fear in - crease; To our cha - os and con -
Church at Pen - te - cost; Help us bear the light of
peace from fields of strife; Bring our bar - ren wastes to
hu - man form made known, Raise us up to be a

fus - ion Let Your light and truth bring peace.
bless - ing To the least, the last, the lost.
blos - som; Lead us out of death to life.
peo - ple Called by love to be Your own.

Text: Carl P. Daw, Jr., b.1944, © 1996, Hope Publishing Co.
Tune: NETTLETON, 8 7 8 7 D; Wyeth's *Repository of Sacred Music, Pt. II*, 1813

42 My Heart Sings Out with Joyful Praise

1. My heart sings out with joy - ful praise To God who
2. The arm of God is strong and just To scat - ter
3. The prom - ise made in a - ges past At last has

rais - es me, Who came to me when I was low
all the proud. The ty - rants tum - ble from their thrones
come to be, For God has come in pow'r to save,

And changed my des - ti - ny. The Ho - ly One, the
And van - ish like a cloud. The hun - gry all are
To set all peo - ple free. Re - mem - b'ring those who

Liv - ing God, Is al - ways full of grace To
sat - is - fied; The rich are sent a - way. The
wait to see Sal - va - tion's dawn - ing day, Our

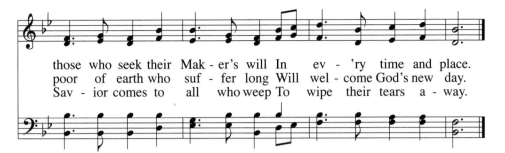

those who seek their Mak - er's will In   ev - 'ry   time and place.
poor   of earth who   suf - fer long Will wel - come God's new day.
Sav - ior comes to   all   who weep To   wipe   their tears a - way.

Text: *Magnificat*, Luke 1:46–55; Ruth Duck, b.1947, © 1992, GIA Publications, Inc.
Tune: CLEANSING FOUNTAIN, 8 6 8 6 D; Early American melody

43 No Trouble at the River

1. I don't want no trou-ble at the riv-er.
2. I don't want no hold up at the riv-er.

I don't want no trou-ble at the riv-er. I don't want no
I don't want no hold up at the riv-er. I don't want no

trou-ble at the riv-er. I don't want no trou-ble at the riv-er.
hold up at the riv-er. I don't want no hold up at the riv-er.

I don't want no trou-ble at the riv-er. I don't want no trou-ble,
I don't want no hold up at the riv-er. I don't want no hold up,

when it's time for me to cross to the oth-er side.
when it's time for me to cross to the oth-er side.

Some-times I feel mis-treat-ed, some-times I feel de-feat-ed, some-

times I feel that I should just give up. But then I think of

Jor-dan. I've got to cross that Jor-dan and I don't want no

D.S.

trou-ble when it's time for me to cross to the oth-er side.

Text: Margaret Pleasant Douroux, b.1941
Tune: Margaret Pleasant Douroux, b.1941
© Rev. Earl Pleasant Publising Co.

44 O Christ, at Your Appearing

1. O Christ, at Your ap - pear - ing The heav - ens rang with song.
2. O Christ, this hour You meet us In sac - ra - men - tal sign.
3. O Christ, ful - fill Your prom - ise; Your king-dom's reign be - gin.
4. O Christ, the world is wait - ing For signs Your reign is near,

That hymn our hearts is cheer-ing As a - ges roll a - long.
You come in love to greet us Through Bread and Word and Wine.
Come, Judge of all the na - tions, And cleanse this world of sin.
While e - vil, un - a - bat - ing, Breeds hope-less-ness and fear.

Though sin and death as - sail us, We claim Your gift of peace.
Lord, grant that we, re - ceiv - ing Your won-drous gifts of grace,
We wait the con-sum - ma - tion Of God's e - ter - nal plan,
Make us Your hands for serv - ice Where peo - ple cry in pain,

Your prom - ise will not fail us Till earth and time shall cease.
Re - joic - ing and be - liev - ing, May leave this ho - ly place.
Pre - pared for all cre - a - tion Since earth and time be - gan.
Your voice for peace and jus - tice Till earth is whole a - gain.

Text: Herman G. Stuempfle, Jr., 1923–2007, © 2000, GIA Publications, Inc.
Tune: SHEFFIELD, 7 6 7 6 D; English melody

1. O Christ, with - in these walls We gath - er 'round Your Word And hear a - gain the prom - ise sure That You are friend and Lord.
2. You feed our hun - gry hearts With fruit of field and vine And share with us Your ris - en life Through gifts of bread and wine.
3. We find our strength re - newed In sol - i - dar - i - ty With sis - ters, broth - ers bound as one In faith and char - i - ty.
4. Then, scat - tered from this place, Un - shelt - ered by these walls, We'll serve a world whose cup of pain For Your com - pas - sion calls.
5. Lord, armed with love and hope, Our fear by faith dis - pelled, We'll bear Your cross till truth pre - vails And jus - tice is up - held.
6. Thus may the Word we hear Be ech - oed where we're sent; And make our acts of serv - ice, Lord, A liv - ing sac - ra - ment.

Text: Herman G. Stuempfle, Jr., 1923–2007, © 1997, GIA Publications, Inc.
Tune: FESTAL SONG, SM; William H. Walter, 1825–1893

46 O God, Whose Healing Power

1. O God, whose heal - ing pow - er Is pres - ent
2. O Christ, who came a - mong us To heal the
3. O Spir - it, ho - ly, heal - ing, De - scend to

ev - 'ry - where, Per - vad - ing all cre - a - tion With
sick, the blind, To bless the poor and bur - dened, The
us to - day. Re - store to all cre - a - tion The

Your e - ter - nal care: Look now in Your com -
bro - ken heart to bind: Send us where they are
peace for which we pray. Re - deem us from the

pas - sion Up - on this world of pain And
wait - ing For hands to help and heal And,
pow - ers That rav - age and de - stroy Till

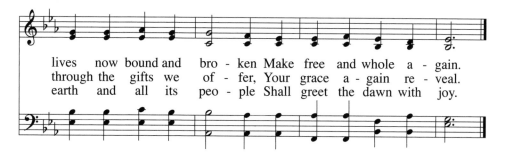

lives now bound and bro - ken Make free and whole a - gain.
through the gifts we of - fer, Your grace a - gain re - veal.
earth and all its peo - ple Shall greet the dawn with joy.

Text: Herman G. Stuempfle, Jr., 1923–2007, © 1997, GIA Publications, Inc.
Tune: AURELIA, 7 6 7 6 D; Samuel Sebastian Wesley, 1810–1876

47　O God, You Are My God Alone

1. O God, You are my God alone, Whom ea - ger - ly I seek, Though long - ing fills my soul with thirst And leaves my bod - y weak. Just like a dry and bar - ren land A-

2. Your faith - ful love sur - pass - es life, E - vok - ing all my praise. Through ev - 'ry day, to bless Your name, My hands in joy I'll raise. My deep - est needs You sat - is - fy As

3. Through - out the night I lie in bed And call You, Lord, to mind; In dark - est hours I med - i - tate How God, my strength, is kind. Be - neath the shad - ow of Your wing, I

waits   a   fresh - 'ning   show'r,   I   long   with - in   Your
with   a   sump - tuous   feast.   So,   on   my   lips   and
live   and feel   se - cure;   And dai - ly   as   I

house   to   see   Your glo - ry   and Your   pow'r.
in   my   heart,   Your praise has nev - er   ceased.
fol - low close,   Your right hand keeps me   sure.

Text: Psalm 63; John L. Bell, b.1949, © 1993, The Iona Community, GIA Publications, Inc., agent
Tune: RESIGNATION, CMD; Funk's *Compilation of Genuine Church Music*, 1832; harm. by John L. Bell, b.1949, © 1993, The Iona Community,
   GIA Publications, Inc., agent

48 O God, Your Word, a Raging Fire

1. O God, Your Word, a rag - ing fire Lies deep with - in our bones. Your truth, a fierce, con - sum - ing pyre; Our flesh, Your al - tar stones.
2. When si - lence burns and faith must speak To crowds who spurn to hear, Your pas - sion's forge will steel the meek; Your love drives out our fear.
3. The an - vil strength with - in Your arm Holds stead - fast, firm and true. When ha - treds strike to cause us harm We rest our trust in You.
4. Your proph - ets felt the scorch - ing breath That spoke Your right - eous will. They bore through per - il, pain, and death— Through threats that threat - en still.
5. O God, Your fire yet keen - ly burns With in our kin - dled hearts. Our call to ra - diant jus - tice yearns To blaze, as grace im - parts!

Text: Mary Louise Bringle, b.1953, © 2002, GIA Publications, Inc.
Tune: ST. ANNE, CM; attr. to William Croft, 1678–1727; harm. composite from 18th C. versions

1. Help me to put not my-self be-fore Thee,
2. Help me to my tongue con - trol,
3. Fix me so that I might do

re - move from my life self-ish - ness and con - ceit;
cleanse me, fill me, make me whole;
on - ly those things that are pleas-ing to You;

Help me the treas-ures of Thy word to seek.
Make me an ex - am - ple to dy - ing souls.
Keep me hum - ble, kind - heart - ed, and true.

O Lord, fix me.
O Lord, fix me.
O Lord, fix me.

Text: Eli Wilson, Jr.
Tune: Eli Wilson, Jr.
© 1983, GIA Publications, Inc.

50   O Radiant Christ, Incarnate Word

1. O ra - diant Christ, in - car - nate Word,
2. Our bar - tered, bus - y lives burn dim,
3. Your glo - ry shone at Jor - dan's stream,
4. O Light of Na - tions, fill the earth;

E - ter - nal love re - vealed in time:
Too tired to care, too numb to feel.
The font where we were born a - new.
Our faith and hope and love re - new.

Come, make Your home with - in our hearts,
Come, shine up - on our shad - owed world:
At - tune Your church to know You near;
Come, lead the peo - ples to Your peace,

That we may dwell in light sub - lime.
Your ra - diance bathes with pow'r to heal.
Il - lu - mine all we say and do.
As stars once led the way to You.

Text: Ruth Duck, b.1947, © 1992, GIA Publications, Inc.
Tune: OLD HUNDREDTH, LM; Louis Bourgeois, c.1510–1561

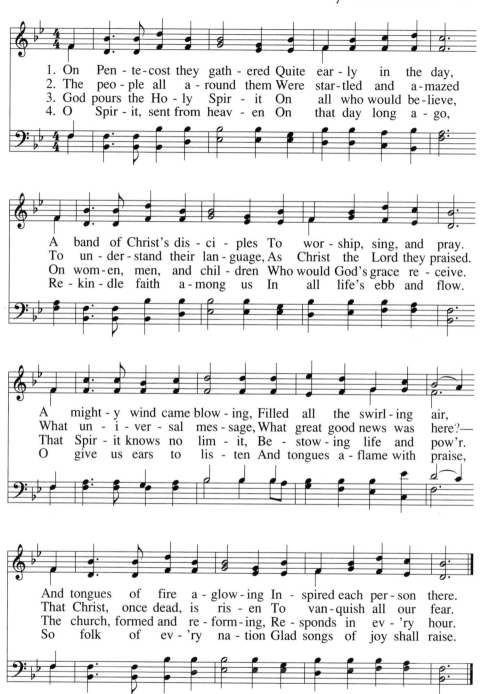

1. On Pen - te-cost they gath - ered Quite ear - ly   in   the day,
2. The peo - ple all a - round them Were star-tled and a-mazed
3. God pours the Ho - ly Spir - it On   all who would be-lieve,
4. O   Spir - it, sent from heav - en On   that day long a - go,

A band of Christ's dis - ci - ples To   wor - ship, sing, and pray.
To un - der-stand their lan-guage, As Christ the Lord they praised.
On wom-en, men, and chil - dren Who would God's grace re - ceive.
Re - kin-dle faith a - mong us In   all life's ebb and flow.

A might - y wind came blow - ing, Filled all   the swirl-ing air,
What un - i - ver - sal mes - sage, What great good news was here?—
That Spir - it knows no lim - it, Be - stow-ing life and pow'r.
O   give us ears to   lis - ten And tongues a-flame with praise,

And tongues of fire a - glow-ing In - spired each per - son there.
That Christ, once dead, is ris - en To van-quish all our fear.
The church, formed and re - form-ing, Re - sponds in ev - 'ry hour.
So   folk   of   ev - 'ry na - tion Glad songs of joy shall raise.

Text: Jane Parker Huber, b.1926, © 1981, admin. by Westminster John Knox Press
Tune: WEBB, 7 6 7 6 D; George J. Webb, 1803–1887

1. Re - buke me not in an - ger, Lord, Nor pun - ish me in wrath. Have pit - y on my weak - ened frame And take the heal - er's path.

2. No long - er wait, but res - cue me; In mer - cy, turn and save. De - liv - er me and spare me from The si - lence of the grave.

3. With moan - ing I grow weak - er still; I flood my bed with tears. My eyes wear out from wea - ri - ness, From end - less griefs and fears.

4. De - part, you e - vil - do - ers all! The Lord has heard my prayers And frus - trates those who trou - ble me, Con - found - ing all their snares.

Text: Psalm 6; Carl P. Daw, Jr., b.1944, © 2005, Hope Publishing Co.
Tune: MAITLAND, CM; George N. Allen, 1812–1877

53 Renew in Me a Right Spirit

Cre - ate in me a clean heart, O Lord;

Re - new in me a right spir - it.

Re - new, re - new, re - new, re - new, re - new in

me a right spir - it.

spir - it.

1. Cast me not a - way from Thee, Let Thy spir - it
2. Give me strength, I want to live to see life grow, to

be in me. Re - store in me the joy I find, sal -
gain, to give. Though al - ways weak, nev - er too strong, with

va - tion free for heart and mind. Re-new, re-new, re-new,
Je - sus there I'll get a - long.

1.
2.

re-new, re-new in me a right spir - it. spir - it.

Text: Psalm 51:10
Tune: Charles Watkins, © 1967; arr. by Frederick D. Stevens, alt.

54 Sing to the Lord

1. Sing to the Lord, who has van - quished the
2. Blessed be Your Name, O God, ev - er our
3. Who can com - pare with Your ho - li - ness,
4. With con - stant love, O God, You set us

horse and the war - rior; Hurled in the
strength and de - fend - er! Snared in the
hon - or and glo - ry? Your won - drous
free and You fed us, Bring - ing us

sea now lies Is - ra - el's scourge and an - noy -
flood, the proud forc - es of Phar - aoh sur - ren -
deeds are the splen - dor of Your peo - ple's sto -
safe - ly to dwell in the land where You led

er! Be glad and sing, For God has done a new
der; Like stones they fall, And the deep swal - lows them
ry: Your might - y arm Saves Your be - lov - ed from
us, Guard - ed by grace, Plant - ed in Your ho - ly

thing;	So	shall	the	Lord reign	for	ev	-	er.
all:	So	shall	the	Lord reign	for	ev	-	er.
harm:	So	shall	the	Lord reign	for	ev	-	er.
place:	So	shall	the	Lord reign	for	ev	-	er.

Text: Carl P. Daw, Jr., b.1944, © 1990, Hope Publishing Co.
Tune: LOBE DEN HERREN, 14 14 47 8; *Stralsund Gesangbuch*, 1665

55 Somebody Here Needs a Blessing

♩ = 53

1. Some-bod-y came to this serv-ice read-y to give up. Some-bod-y came to this serv-ice, say-ing, "Lord, I've had e-nough. Some-bod-y in the build-ing wants to be free.

2. Some-bod-y came to this serv-ice with trou-ble on their mind. Fi-nan-ces low, no place to go and their bills are all be-hind.

Some-bod-y in the build-ing needs the vic - to-ry.

Some-bod-y here needs a touch, some-bod-y here needs a

mir-a-cle. Some-bod-y here needs a bless-ing,

Last time

right now, right now, right now.

Last time

Touch, Lord, touch, Lord, touch, Lord, touch, Lord!

D.S.

Touch, Lord, touch, Lord, touch, Lord, touch, Lord!

Text: Eddie A. Robinson
Tune: Eddie A. Robinson
© 2006, Eddie A. Robinson

The Lamps of Evening (Vesper Hymn)   56

1. The lamps of ev - 'ning burn at close of day,
2. Fill Thou each need - ful want, each prayer in - spire,
3. Em - brace our loved ones in Thy ten - der care,

With - in Thy tem - ple, Lord, we come to pray.
Kin - dle a flame of love and pure de - sire:
Guide and sus - tain them where - so - e'er they fare.

Light Thou the tem - ple of our hearts with - in,
Sup - port the weak, en - cour - age Thou the strong,
Be Thou the Shep - herd of all pil - grim feet,

Let grace de - scend and songs of praise be - gin.
Bind us in kind - ly serv - ice as in song.
Till at Thy ev - er - last - ing throne we meet.

Text: Karl Reiland, 1871–1964
Tune: TOULON, 10 10 10 10; adapt. from OLD 124th, *Genevan Psalter*, 1551; arr. by Harry T. Burleigh, 1866–1949; © 2007, GIA Publications, Inc.

57   The Lord's Prayer

Our Fa-ther, who art in heav'n, hal-lowed be Thy name. Thy

king-dom come, Thy will be done on earth as it is in heav'n. Give

us this day our dai-ly bread, and for - give us our

tress - pass-es, our tres - pass-es, as we for - give those who

tress - pass a-gainst us.   And lead us not in - to temp -

Music: Harry T. Burleigh, 1866–1949, © 2007, GIA Publications, Inc.

The Thirsty Cry for Water, Lord 58

1. The thirst - y cry for wa - ter, Lord; The
2. The cup of wa - ter poured in love The
3. But help us al - so hear the cry Of
4. And come to us, O ris - en Christ, Our

hun - gry plead for bread. And man - y long to
pangs of thirst will still. The bread of earth You
hun - g'ring, thirst - ing hearts For liv - ing wa - ter,
rest - less souls re - lieve; And sat - is - fy our

rise a - gain Where hope, cast down, lies dead.
bid us share, The fam - ished child can fill.
bread of life Your grace a - lone im - parts.
starv - ing hearts That we may rise and live.

Text: John 4:5–42; Herman G. Stuempfle, Jr., 1923–2007, © 1997, GIA Publications, Inc.
Tune: NEW BRITAIN, CM; *Virginia Harmony*, 1831; harm. by Edwin O. Excell, 1851–1921

59 The World of Forms and Changes

1. The world of forms and chang-es Is just now
2. Old Sa - tan tries to throw down { Ev - 'ry -
3. There are some men and wom - en That help the
4. If the preach - er in his ser - mon, Stands up to
5. I know we have too man - y Who are liv - ing
6. Our boast - ed land and na - tion, Are plung-ing
7. There is a land of prom - ise, Where tri - als

so con - fused, That there is found some dan - ger In
thing that's good; He'd fix a way to con - found The
dev - il on By con - stant - ly com - plain - ing Of
tell the truth, They'll go a - bout and mur - mur, With
in the dark; They have but lit - tle if an - y, Of
in dis - grace; With pic - tures of star - va - tion Al -
are un - known, Where Sa - tan nev - er com - eth, For

ev - 'ry - thing you use; But this is con - so -
right - eous if he could. But thanks to God Al -
ev - 'ry - thing that's done, They want to be called
slan - der and a - buse, They want the whole ar -
Chris - tian work at heart, But thous - ands, though 'tis
most in ev - 'ry place; While loads of need - ed
God is on the throne; And just a lit - tle

la - tion | To ev - 'ry blood - washed child: | The
might - y | That he can - not be - guile; | And
Chris - tians | And all their bad - ness hide; | God
range - ment | To suit their self - ish style; | But
storm - y, | Are march - ing un - de - filed; | And
mon - ey, | Re - main in hoard - ed piles; | But
long - er, | By faith and self - de - nial, | We'll

Lord will change our na - tion, af - ter a - while.
we will be done fight - ing, af - ter a - while.
will o - pen the se - cret, af - ter a - while.
God will sit in judg - ment, af - ter a - while.
God will head the ar - my, af - ter a - while.
God will rule this coun - try, af - ter a - while.
join our friends up yon - der, af - ter a - while.

Af - ter a - while, af - ter a - while, the

Lord will change our sta - tion, af - ter a - while.

Text: Charles A. Tindley, 1851–1933
Tune: FORMS AND CHANGES, 7 6 7 6 7 6 7 4 with refrain; Charles A. Tindley, 1851–1933

This page has been intentionally left blank.

1. To God com-pose a song of joy; To
2. Be - fore the na - tions God re - veals A
3. In ev - 'ry cor - ner of the earth, God
4. With trum - pet, with the sound of horns, With
5. Let seas in all their full - ness roar; Sing,
6. The God of jus - tice comes to save; Let

God make mel - o - dy, Whose arm of strength does
just and right - eous will, Re - mem - ber - ing in
comes to save and free; Break forth with shouts of
strings, yes, with the lyre, With voic - es praise the
peo - ple of all lands; Let moun-tains join and
earth make mel - o - dy; For God will judge with

won - drous things, Whose hand brings vic - to - ry!
faith - ful love The house of Is - ra - el.
ho - ly joy; All lands, make mel - o - dy.
sov - 'reign God, A lus - ty, joy - ous choir.
shout for joy; Let riv - ers clap their hands.
right - eous - ness And rule with eq - ui - ty.

Text: Psalm 98; Ruth Duck, b.1947, © 1992, GIA Publications, Inc.
Tune: AZMON, CM; Carl G. Gläser, 1784-1829; harm. by Lowell Mason, 1792-1872

61 Tomorrow Christ Is Coming

1. To - mor - row Christ is com - ing As
2. To - mor - row will be Christ - mas, The
3. There will be no to - mor - rows For
4. Our God be - comes in - car - nate In

yes - ter - day He came; A child is born this
feast of love di - vine, But for the name - less
man - y a ba - by born. Good Fri - day falls on
ev - 'ry hu - man birth. Cre - at - ed in God's

mo - ment— We do not know its name. The
mil - lions The star will nev - er shine. Still
Christ - mas When life is sown as corn. But
im - age, We must make peace on earth. God

world is full of dark - ness, A -
is the cen - sus tak - en With
Je - sus Christ is ris - en And
will ful - fil Love's pur - pose And

gain there is no room; The sym-bols of ex -
peo - ple on the move; New in - fants born in
comes a - gain in bread To still our deep - est
this shall be the sign: We shall find Christ a -

is - tence Are sta - ble, cross and tomb.
sta - bles Are cry - ing out for love.
hun - ger And raise us from the dead.
mong us As wom - an, child or man.

Text: Fred Kaan, b.1929, © 1968, Hope Publishing Co.
Tune: PASSION CHORALE, 7 6 7 6 D; Hans Leo Hassler, 1564–1612; harm. by J. S. Bach, 1685–1750

We stud - y,   we shout,   we

serve!

Text: Eddie A. Robinson
Tune: Eddie A. Robinson
© 2006, Eddie A. Robinson

63 When Illness Meets Denial and Rejection

1. When ill-ness meets de - ni - al and re - jec - tion,
2. For - give Your Chur-ch's sear - ing, numb - ing si - lence,
3. Help us re - sist, re - fuse all venge - ful nam - ing
4. Show us our hid - den strength and hu - man lim - its.
5. Give us, a - mid our pas - sion and per - sis - tence,
6. Through sum - mer joys, and win - ters of de - jec - tion,

When friends re - coil, and fac - es turn to stone,
Un - ho - ly hud - dles, mud - dles and de - lays.
Of lep - ers, plagues, and pun - ish - ment for sin,
Free us from guilt, self - ha - tred and de - spair,
The peace that wish - ful think - ing can - not fake.
Help us, by faith, to trav - el, weep and sing,

Christ of our Sor - rows, raise us from de - ject - ion,
For - give our zeal to hide the fear that drives us
With love's de - term - ined pow'r to ban - ish blam - ing,
To cel - e - brate, as flesh - em - bod - ied spir - its,
Link us in lov - ing cir - cles of re - sis - tance,
With hearts that reap the fruit of res - ur - rec - tion,

To trav - el on, as - sailed but not a - lone.
With harsh, un - lov - ing words, un - heal - ing ways.
Shed light and truth, and heal the hurt with - in.
Our bod - y's beau - ty, and our Mak - er's care.
With love of life that death can nev - er break.
And hands that bear the lov - ing touch of spring.

Text: Brian Wren, b.1936, © 1996, Hope Publishing Co.
Tune: O PERFECT LOVE, 11 10 11 10; Joseph Barnby, 1838–1896

64 When Memory Fades

1. When mem-'ry fades and rec-og-ni-tion fal-ters,
2. As frail-ness grows, and youth-ful strengths di-min-ish
3. With-in Your Spir-it, good-ness lives un-fad-ing.

When eyes we love grow dim, and minds, con-fused,
In wea-ry arms, which worked their ear-nest fill,
The past and fu-ture min-gle in-to one.

Speak to our souls of love that nev-er al-ters;
Your ag-ing ser-vants la-bor now to fin-ish
All joys re-main, un-shad-owed light per-vad-ing.

Speak to our hearts by pain and fear a-bused.
Their earth-ly tasks, as fits Your mys-tery's will.
No val-ued deed will ev-er be un-done.

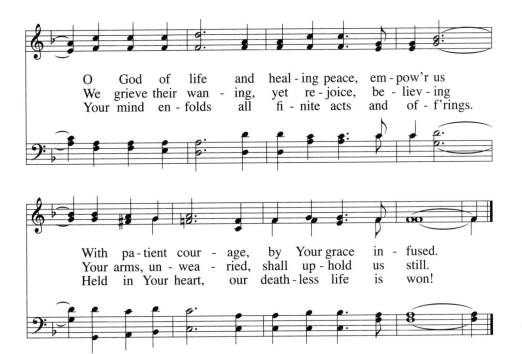

O God of life and heal-ing peace, em-pow'r us
We grieve their wan - ing, yet re-joice, be - liev-ing
Your mind en-folds all fi - nite acts and of - f'rings.

With pa-tient cour - age, by Your grace in - fused.
Your arms, un - wea - ried, shall up-hold us still.
Held in Your heart, our death-less life is won!

Text: Mary Louise Bringle, b.1953, © 2002, GIA Publications, Inc.
Tune: FINLANDIA, 11 10 11 10 11 10; Jean Sibelius, 1865–1957

65 When Minds and Bodies Meet as One

1. When minds and bod - ies meet as one And
2. When lead - ers meet with an - gry sound, Yet
3. When team - work serves a com - mon aim And
4. When peo - ple feel the lash - ing claws Of
5. In Christ we come to break and bless The

find their true af - fin - i - ty, We join the dance in
bri - dle their hos - til - i - ty To bar - gain for a
play - ers move in sym - pa - thy, The flow - ing rhy - thm
greed and in - hu - man - i - ty, Yet strug - gle in a
bread of new so - ci - e - ty, Cre - at - ed for to -

God be - gun And move with - in the Trin - i - ty,
com - mon ground And end with u - na - nim - i - ty,
of the game Is beau - ty in sim - plic - i - ty,
right - ful cause With love and sol - i - dar - i - ty,
geth - er - ness From in - fi - nite va - ri - e - ty,

So praise the good that's seen and done In lov - ing, giv - ing
Be glad for all the hope that's won In ev - 'ry gleam of
So praise the good that's seen and done In swift - ly mov - ing
Be glad for all the hope that's won In free - dom - lov - ing
So praise the good that's seen and done In Spir - it - giv - en

u - ni - ty, Re - veal - ing God, for - ev - er One,
u - ni - ty, Re - veal - ing God, for - ev - er One,
u - ni - ty, Re - veal - ing God, for - ev - er One,
u - ni - ty, Re - veal - ing God, for - ev - er One,
u - ni - ty, Re - veal - ing God, for - ev - er One,

Whose na - ture is Com - mu - ni - ty.
Whose na - ture is Com - mu - ni - ty.
Whose na - ture is Com - mu - ni - ty.
Whose na - ture is Com - mu - ni - ty.
Whose na - ture is Com - mu - ni - ty.

Text: Brian Wren, b.1936, © 1980, Hope Publishing Co.
Tune: SWEET HOUR, LMD; William B. Bradbury, 1816–1868

1. When ter - ror streaks through morn - ing skies And
2. Come reach us through the mute ap - peal Of
3. Through ash and rub - ble of our past, You
4. Re - deem - ing God, when ha - treds turn Our

fear - dazed minds grow numb, With in - ter - ced - ing,
dust - smeared hands and face, Whose acts of val - iant
held our hopes a - lone. Re - build our fra - gile
morn - ing skies to night, Trans - form our rag - ing

prayer - ful sighs, O Heal - ing Spir - it, come.
love re - veal An un - ex - pect - ed grace.
dreams to last: Of faith and not of stone.
hearts to yearn For peace and heal - ing light.

Text: Mary Louise Bringle, b.1953, © 2002, GIA Publications, Inc.
Tune: MORNING SONG, 8 6 8 6 8 6; *Kentucky Harmony*, 1816; harm. by C. Winfred Douglas, 1867–1944, © 1940, The Church Pension Fund

Two days after the events of September 11, 2001, Mary Louise Bringle penned this text. It is at once a lament, an intercession, and a thanksgiving for the courageous acts of rescue workers.

67 Wind of the Spirit

1. Wind of the Spir - it, blow a - cross cre - a - tion.
2. Flame of the Spir - it, burn with truth's clear judg - ment,
3. Dove of the Spir - it, fly through all the a - ges.

Breathe as You did when cha - os first held sway.
Purg - ing, re - fin - ing by Your search - ing Word.
Prom - ise of peace shines bright - ly on Your wings.

Come, fierce as tem - pest, swirl - ing forth and sweep - ing
Melt down the walls of hate that still di - vide us.
Gen - tly but swift - ly, on You soar un - rest - ing,

All that de - fies Your vast de - sign a - way.
Forge us and form us as Your liv - ing sword
Call - ing un - til the choir of na - tions sings,

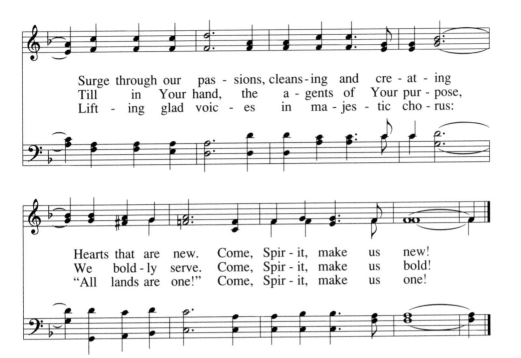

Surge through our pas - sions, cleans - ing and cre - at - ing
Till in Your hand, the a - gents of Your pur - pose,
Lift - ing glad voic - es in ma - jes - tic cho - rus:

Hearts that are new. Come, Spir - it, make us new!
We bold - ly serve. Come, Spir - it, make us bold!
"All lands are one!" Come, Spir - it, make us one!

Text: Herman G. Stuempfle, Jr., 1923–2007, © 1997, GIA Publications, Inc.
Tune: FINLANDIA, 11 10 11 10 11 10; Jean Sibelius, 1865–1957

68 With Humble Justice Clad and Crowned

1. With hum-ble jus-tice clad and crowned, The
2. The Word of truth will free the op-pressed, And,
3. As thun-der-clouds of love rain down Life-
4. Say not that jus-tice nev-er dawns, That

Christ of God will come a-gain And sing in ev-'ry
just-ly judg-ing ev-'ry need, Will end the pow'r of
giv-ing, u-ni-ver-sal show'rs, The meek will rule, and
peace on earth will nev-er come. The prom-ise shines from

land on earth The song be-gun at Beth-le-hem,
flaunt-ed wealth, And cru-el, quiet, sys-tem-ic greed.
thus re-deem Earth's high au-thor-i-ties and pow'rs,
Beth-le-hem, For all, for-ev-er, like the sun.

And jus-tice shall de-fend the poor As barn and ware-house
The vi-o-lence of self-ish lust To have and hold at
As work-ers dance with heads of state, And all u-nite, em-
A-long the high-way of the weak, The poor-est and the

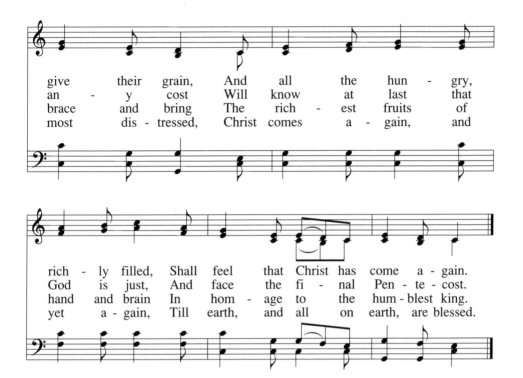

give   their   grain,   And   all   the   hun - gry,
an   -   y   cost   Will   know   at   last   that
brace   and   bring   The   rich -   est   fruits   of
most   dis - tressed,   Christ   comes   a - gain,   and

rich - ly   filled,   Shall   feel   that   Christ   has   come a - gain.
God   is   just,   And   face   the   fi - nal   Pen - te - cost.
hand   and   brain   In   hom - age   to   the   hum - blest king.
yet   a - gain,   Till   earth,   and   all   on   earth,   are blessed.

Text: Brian Wren, b.1936, © 1993, Hope Publishing Co.
Tune: SWEET HOUR, LMD; William B. Bradbury, 1816–1868

69 Woe to the Prophets

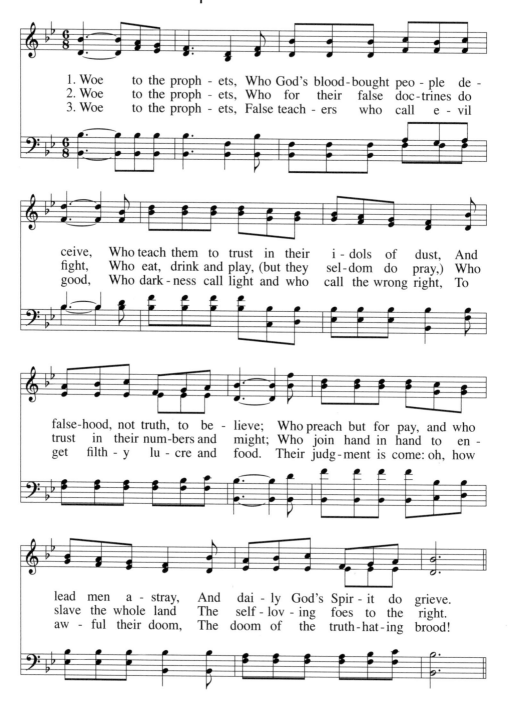

1. Woe to the proph - ets, Who God's blood - bought peo - ple de -
ceive, Who teach them to trust in their i - dols of dust, And
false - hood, not truth, to be - lieve; Who preach but for pay, and who
lead men a - stray, And dai - ly God's Spir - it do grieve.

2. Woe to the proph - ets, Who for their false doc - trines do
fight, Who eat, drink and play, (but they sel - dom do pray,) Who
trust in their num - bers and might; Who join hand in hand to en -
slave the whole land The self - lov - ing foes to the right.

3. Woe to the proph - ets, False teach - ers who call e - vil
good, Who dark - ness call light and who call the wrong right, To
get filth - y lu - cre and food. Their judg - ment is come: oh, how
aw - ful their doom, The doom of the truth - hat - ing brood!

Woe, woe, woe! How fast to the judg-ment they go! No God and no hope, In dark-ness they grope, By pas-sion and greed, by hab-it and need Bound hard un-to sin, No Sav-ior with-in, To judg-ment, to judg-ment they go.

Text: Charles P. Jones, 1865–1949
Tune: WOE TO THE PROPHETS, 5 8 11 8 11 8 with refrain; Charles P. Jones, 1865–1949

70 You Call Us to the Feast

1. You call us to the feast Where You pre -
2. Be - cause You bid us come, With rev - 'rence
3. Lord, grant us hum - bled hearts That know their
4. Re - ceive our thanks, O Christ, For gifts You

side with grace. In bro - ken bread and
we draw near. We long to share this
guilt and loss, And fill our emp - ty,
here sup - ply— Our life re - newed, our

of - fered cup You meet us face to face.
meal with You, Your Word of prom - ise hear.
wait - ing hands With to - kens of Your cross.
hope re - stored Through love that can - not die.

Text: Herman G. Stuempfle, Jr., 1923–2007, © 1997, GIA Publications, Inc.
Tune: DENNIS, SM; John G. Nägeli, 1773–1836; arr. by Lowell Mason, 1792–1872

71 You, Lord, Are Both Lamb and Shepherd

Unison

1. You, Lord, are both Lamb and Shep - herd. You, Lord,
2. Clothed in light up - on the moun - tain, Stripped of
3. You, who walk each day be - side us, Sit in
4. Wor - thy is our earth - ly Je - sus! Wor - thy

are both prince and slave. You, peace-mak - er
might up - on the cross, Shin - ing in e -
pow - er at God's side. You, who preach a
is our cos - mic Christ! Wor - thy Your de -

and sword - bring - er Of the way You
ter - nal glo - ry, Beg - gar'd by a
way that's nar - row, Have a love that
feat and vic - t'ry. Wor - thy still Your

took and gave. You, the ev - er - last - ing
sol - dier's toss, You, the ev - er - last - ing
reach - es wide. You, the ev - er - last - ing
peace and strife. You, the ev - er - last - ing

in - stant; You, whom we both scorn and crave.
in - stant; You, who are our gift and cost.
in - stant; You, who are our pil - grim guide.
in - stant; You, who are our death and life.

Text: Sylvia Dunstan, 1955–1993, © 1991, GIA Publications, Inc.
Tune: PICARDY, 8 7 8 7 8 7; French Carol; harm. by Richard Proulx, b.1937, © 1986, GIA Publications, Inc.

Alternate tune: REGENT SQUARE, no. 20.

72   Acknowledgments

2 Text: © 1958, Estate of C. Eric Lincoln. Tune: © 1981, Estate of J. Jefferson Cleveland

3 Text: © 1992, GIA Publications, Inc.

4 Text: © 2006, GIA Publications, Inc.

5 Text: © 2001, Hope Publishing Company, Carol Stream, IL 60188. All rights reserved. Used by permission.

6 Text: © 1975, rev. 1995, Hope Publishing Company, Carol Stream, IL 60188. All rights reserved. Used by permission.

7 Text: © 2006, GIA Publications, Inc.

8 Text: © 1986, Jane Parker Huber. Admin. by Westminster John Knox Press

9 Text: © 1992, Hope Publishing Company, Carol Stream, IL 60188. All rights reserved. Used by permission.

10 Text: © 1996, Hope Publishing Company, Carol Stream, IL 60188. All rights reserved. Used by permission.

12 © Rev. Earl Pleasant Publishing Co.

13 Text: © 1996, Hope Publishing Company, Carol Stream, IL 60188. All rights reserved. Used by permission. Tune: © 1983, GIA Publications, Inc.

14 Text and tune: © 1981, Rev. Earl Pleasant Publishing Co. Arr. © 2007, GIA Publications, Inc.

15 Text: © 1968, Hope Publishing Company, Carol Stream, IL 60188. All rights reserved. Used by permission.

16 Text: © 1992, Hope Publishing Company, Carol Stream, IL 60188. All rights reserved. Used by permission.

18 Text: © 1991, GIA Publications, Inc.

19 Text: © 2006, GIA Publications, Inc. Arr.: © 2000, GIA Publications, Inc.

20 Text: © 1992, Hope Publishing Company, Carol Stream, IL 60188. All rights reserved. Used by permission.

21 Text: © 2002, GIA Publications, Inc.

22 Text: © 1984, Jane Parker Huber. Admin. by Westminster John Knox Press

23 Text: © 1984, Jane Parker Huber. Admin. by Westminster John Knox Press

24 Text: © 1997, Hope Publishing Company, Carol Stream, IL 60188. All rights reserved. Used by permission.

25 Text: 1992, GIA Publications, Inc.

26 Text: © 1975, Hope Publishing Company, Carol Stream, IL 60188. All rights reserved. Used by permission.

27 Text: © 1997, GIA Publications, Inc.

28 Text: © 1989, Hope Publishing Company, Carol Stream, IL 60188. All rights reserved. Used by permission.

29 Text: © 1993, GIA Publications, Inc.

30 Text: © 1989, Hope Publishing Company, Carol Stream, IL 60188. All rights reserved. Used by permission.

31 © Jimmy Dowell

32 Text: © 1971, rev. 1995, Hope Publishing Company, Carol Stream, IL 60188. All rights reserved. Used by permission.

33 © 1965, 1973, Laymon T. Hunter

34 Text: © 2000, Kevin Mayhew Ltd., Buxhall, Stowmarket, IP14 3B W, UK. Reproduced by permission, Licence no. 704081/3. (www.kevinmayhewltd.com)

35 Text: © 1992, Hope Publishing Company, Carol Stream, IL 60188. All rights reserved. Used by permission.

37 Text: © 1992, GIA Publications, Inc.

38 Text: © 2002, GIA Publications, Inc. Tune: © 1942, Ren. 1970, Hope Publishing Company, Carol Stream, IL 60188. All rights reserved. Used by permission.

39 Text: © 1997, GIA Publications, Inc.

41 Text: © 1996, Hope Publishing Company, Carol Stream, IL 60188. All rights reserved. Used by permission.

42 Text: © 1992, GIA Publications, Inc.

43 © Rev. Earl Pleasant Publising Co.

44 Text: © 2000, GIA Publications, Inc.

45 Text: © 1997, GIA Publications, Inc.

46 Text: © 1997, GIA Publications, Inc.

47 Text and harm.: © 1993, The Iona Community, GIA Publications, Inc., agent

48 Text: © 2002, GIA Publications, Inc.

49 © 1983, GIA Publications, Inc.

50 Text: © 1992, GIA Publications, Inc.

51 Text: © 1981, Jane Parker Huber. Admin. by Westminster John Knox Press

52 Text: © 2005, Hope Publishing Company, Carol Stream, IL 60188. All rights reserved. Used by permission.

53 © 1967, Charles Watkins

54 Text: © 1990, Hope Publishing Company, Carol Stream, IL 60188. All rights reserved. Used by permission.

55 © 2006, Eddie A. Robinson

58 Text: © 1997, GIA Publications, Inc.

60 Text: © 1992, GIA Publications, Inc.

61 Text: © 1968, Hope Publishing Company, Carol Stream, IL 60188. All rights reserved. Used by permission.

62 © 2006, Eddie A. Robinson

63 Text: © 1993, Hope Publishing Company, Carol Stream, IL 60188. All rights reserved. Used by permission.

64 Text: © 2002, GIA Publications, Inc.

65 Text: © 1980, Hope Publishing Company, Carol Stream, IL 60188. All rights reserved. Used by permission.

66 Text: © 2002, GIA Publications, Inc. Arr.: © 1940, The Church Pension Fund. Used by permission of Church Publishing Incorporated, New York.

67 Text: © 1997, GIA Publications, Inc.

68 Text: © 1993, Hope Publishing Company, Carol Stream, IL 60188. All rights reserved. Used by permission.

70 Text: © 1997, GIA Publications, Inc.

71 Text: © 1991, GIA Publications, Inc. Harm.: © 1986, GIA Publications, Inc.

73 Topical Index

Topical Index/*continued*

Topical Index/*continued*

Topical Index/*continued*

SM
- 70 DENNIS
- 45 FESTAL SONG
- 29 TRENTHAM

CM
- 27 ARLINGTON
- 10 60 AZMON
- 52 MAITLAND
- 19 MARTYRDOM
- 39 McKEE
- 66 MORNING SONG
- 25 58 NEW BRITAIN
- 48 ST. ANNE

CM WITH REPEAT
- 32 CORONATION

CMD
- 47 RESIGNATION

LM
- 6 DUKE STREET
- 30 50 OLD 100th
- 28 WOODWORTH

LMD
- 65 68 SWEET HOUR

5 8 11 8 11 8 WITH REFRAIN
- 69 WOE TO THE PROPHETS

7 6 7 6 D
- 26 46 AURELIA
- 37 LANCASHIRE
- 61 PASSION CHORALE
- 44 SHEFFIELD
- 51 WEBB

7 6 8 6 D WITH REFRAIN
- 1 A BETTER DAY

7 6 7 6 7 6 7 4 WITH REFRAIN
- 59 FORMS AND CHANGES

7 7 7 7 7 7
- 13 JULION

8 6 8 6 D
- 42 CLEANSING FOUNTAIN

8 7 8 7 D
- 38 ABBOT'S LEIGH
- 21 ALL THE WAY
- 3 BEECHER
- 9 CONVERSE
- 34 EBENEZER
- 22 24 HYFRYDOL
- 7 16 23 HYMN TO JOY
- 5 41 NETTLETON

8 7 8 7 WITH REFRAIN
- 4 BRYN CALFARIA
- 17 GLORIFY HIS NAME
- 36 JESUS ONLY

8 7 8 7 8 7
- 71 PICARDY
- 20 REGENT SQUARE

8 7 8 7 8 77
- 15 35 CWM RHONDDA

10 10 10 10
- 8 NATIONAL HYMN
- 56 TOULON

10 10 10 WITH ALLELUIAS
- 18 SINE NOMINE

11 10 11 10
- 63 PERFECT LOVE

11 10 11 10 11 10
- 64 67 FINLANDIA

11 11 11 9 WITH REFRAIN
- 40 LOVE ONE ANOTHER

11 11 11 11 WITH REFRAIN
- 11 COME UNTO ME

14 14 47 8
- 54 LOBE DEN HERREN

First Line and Common Title Index/*continued*